PRAISE FOR BEYOND CHAMPIONSHIPS TEEN EDITION

Coach Dru has shared some valuable principles in life with us in *Beyond Championships*. My son, Jibri, came to Coach Dru's program at St. Vincent-St. Mary as a junior in high school and has become a better person and a better player. I am grateful for Coach Dru's mentoring and the leadership he is providing for so many young people. *Beyond Championships* reveals the heart and soul of a good man and a good coach. It's a must-read for young people, as well as for older people. Thanks, Coach Dru, for sharing with us some lifetime lessons we can all use on our journey.

> *Mel Blount, four-time Super Bowl champ and member of the NFL Hall of Fame*

After graduating from high school, the number one question I received was, "What was it like playing with LeBron?" The second most-asked question was, "What kind of coach did you have?" The first question was easier to answer than the second. But now you can read this book and begin to understand how great a man Coach Dru is! For Coach Dru, living a full and productive life has always been about more than just basketball. It's about relationships and being a Christian man and being a great father. It's about how to treat women, how to compete, how to be a student athlete, and so much more. Coach Dru is the best coach I've ever had. Not just because he's so good at the X's and O's, but also because he knows how to help a young person be the best person he can be. Coach often asked, "Are you prepared for the game of life? Because it never stops, even when the clock on the scoreboard hits 00:00!" Thank you, Coach Dru, for all you have done to prepare me for the game of life.

> *Willie McGee, "Fab Five" member of the St. Vincent-St. Mary basketball team (1999–2003) and current assistant coach of the Chowan University men's basketball team*

One of my favorite maxims is "serve the underserved," and few people put these words into practice like Coach Dru Joyce does. We all know the incredible work he did in helping LeBron James develop into the player and, more importantly, the individual he's become. I'm excited that in *Beyond Championships*, Coach Dru shares the principles that helped mold so many other young lives as well. Coach Dru's story should inspire all readers, both young and old alike, to have the faith to chase their dreams, no matter what obstacles they perceive to be in front of them.

> *Russell Simmons, cofounder of Def Jam Records*
> *and author of* Super Rich: A Guide to Having It All

Anything that Dru Joyce has to say is important, because he is a quality man who cares about young men!

> *Bishop F. Josephus Johnson II, presiding bishop of*
> *The Beth-El Fellowship of Visionary Churches and*
> *senior pastor of The House of the Lord*

Coach Dru's teachings on faith, family, and character are an inspiration to athletes and nonathletes alike. *Beyond Championships* transcends sports the way Coach Dru's influence on young lives reaches far beyond the basketball court.

> *Kristopher Belman, writer/director of the documentary*
> More Than a Game

Beyond Championships is what happens when one of the nation's most influential high school coaches lets us in on his secrets to success. Whether or not you love sports, this book and the life lessons herein are invaluable to both young and old. Sit down, read, enjoy, and learn!

> *Harvey Mason Jr., music/movie producer; producer*
> *of* More Than a Game

Beyond Championships

Teen Edition

A PLAYBOOK FOR
WINNING AT LIFE

BY COACH DRU JOYCE II

with Chris Morrow

ZONDERVAN

Beyond Championships Teen Edition
Copyright © 2015 by James Dru Joyce II

This title is also available as a Zondervan ebook. Visit www.zondervan.com/ebooks.

Requests for information should be addressed to:
Zondervan, 3900 Sparks Dr. SE, Grand Rapids, Michigan 49546

ISBN: 978-0-310-74615-7

The editors would like to thank Jesse Florea for his significant and notable contributions to this work.

Cover design: Cindy Davis
Cover photography or illustration: Dan Davis Photography
Photo insert: All photos courtesy of Coach Dru Joyce II unless otherwise noted
Photo insert background: ©tothzoli001 / Shutterstock
Interior photography: ©moomsabuy / Shutterstock®, ©tothzoli001 / Shutterstock®
Interior and photo insert design: Kait Lamphere

Printed in the United States of America

15 16 17 18 19 20 21 /DCI/ 20 19 18 17 16 15 14 13 12 11 10 9 8 7 6 5 4 3 2 1

To Carolyn, my wife,
life couldn't have given me a better soul mate
and partner. You have challenged and inspired me to
always be better. You most likely could have done
well in life without me, but I know I could
have never made it without you.

With all my love,
Dru

TABLE OF CONTENTS

FOREWORD BY LEBRON JAMES

It's hard to believe now, but I was close to the same age my son is today when I first met Coach Dru.

As a young kid in Akron, Ohio, I was like a lot of other kids. I wanted to play basketball and hang out with my friends. So when Coach Dru asked me to play on his team, at the time it was all about basketball. But looking back on it, I now know there was something far greater at work that made me walk into that dusty Salvation Army gym in Akron. Because as much as I wanted to learn and play basketball, what I needed at that point in my life was someone who could show me more than just the X's and O's. Coach Dru taught me about life.

Being raised by a single mom, I knew it was important that I had a male presence in my life — men I could look up to and go to for direction. Prior to meeting Coach Dru, Frank Walker gave me that guidance. When Coach Dru came along, my support system grew, and I related to him on a different level — he knew what it meant to be poor, a feeling I was already too familiar with as a ten-year-old. Most importantly, he knew how to transcend his circumstances, and he wanted to share that knowledge with us too.

That's why I'm so excited for this book. I know firsthand how well these principles work. They worked for me and my brothers — Dru, Sian, Willie, and Romeo — growing up in Akron. My brothers and I were no different from other kids all over the world. We all had dreams. For too many kids, those dreams feel unreachable. But for us, they never did. Because Coach Dru showed us that no matter what sort of obstacles we faced, we could make our dreams a reality.

There are a lot of principles in this book that have become cornerstones of my own philosophy on life. But the principle that has probably impacted me the most is *to always have the heart of a servant.* That's something I learned from Coach Dru, and in many ways it was at the heart of my decision to return to Northeast Ohio as a basketball player.

On the court, the goal will always be to win a title. But off the court, the more important goal remains to shape the lives of young people in the community in the same way that Coach Dru shaped mine. And if I can do that, even just a little bit, then I will have accomplished something that means so much more to me than any championship.

LeBron James,
August 2014

INTRODUCTION

This book has very little to do with actual basketball. Yes, stories about basketball fill these pages. But my desire isn't for you to become a better basketball player. Instead, my aim is to pass along a series of principles that helped me become who I am today. These principles armed me on my own journey and helped me guide numerous groups of talented boys into manhood.

These same principles can shape and change your destiny as well. As you move through the chapters of this book, you'll discover:

- that your *Decisions Create Environment*[1]
- the *Power of Words*
- *The Myth of the Self-Made Man*
- how to *Use the Game, Don't Let the Game Use You*
- that *Discipline Determines Your Destiny*
- how important it is to have the *Heart of a Servant*
- that in the midst of life's difficulties you must *Make Lemonade*
- the ways to *Take Charge of Your Mind*
- and the power that comes by *Daring to Dream*

I grew up with football as my passion. But ever since my son, Dru III, fell in love with basketball at a young age, I've grown to share his opinion of the sport. I coached Lil' Dru (that's what everybody called him) and his friends through American Athletic Union (AAU) basketball and became an assistant coach at St. Vincent-St. Mary High School in Akron, Ohio, when he was a freshman. Two years later, in 2001, it was my honor to take over as head coach for the STVM Fighting Irish.

Maybe you already know St. Vincent-St. Mary as one of the best basketball schools in the country. LeBron James played his high school ball there, and I was his coach. Before the hype, before the fame and riches, before the posters, before he was "King James," a much younger (and smaller) LeBron would hang out at my house with the rest of the team.

But this is also not a book about LeBron James. Yes, stories about him take up part of this text. But it's not like LeBron is on the phone with me every night discussing strategy or his last game. No, there are folks who are way more qualified than I am for that in his life now. But our connection runs deep. To hear someone like LeBron — who has accomplished so much while overcoming so much — say, "You're my role model," for me that's the ultimate, knowing that I've had a major impact on who he is.

And to be clear, I'm not talking about LeBron's jump shot here, or how he plays defense. My impact on LeBron's life can't be quantified in X's and O's. Instead, if he's taken anything of lasting value from our relationship, it's how to carry himself through life, as a man, husband, and father.

I remember being in a restaurant with the team after a game we played at the Palestra, the historic arena at the University of Pennsylvania, during LeBron's senior year. He walked over to the table where my wife and I sat and announced that one day he wanted to be just like Mrs. Joyce and me. And now he is a loving husband and a doting father. He treats his wife with respect and love. He's there for his children. I like to believe he learned a lot of that from watching us.

So what is this book? My hope is that it will resonate with anyone searching for ways to build character and overcome struggles, regardless of religion, race, sex, or station in life. By hearing some of the hardships I have faced, alongside the principles that pulled me out of them, this book can serve as a blueprint for *anyone* looking to make better choices and reach their full potential.

Coach Dru Joyce

CHAPTER 1

Coming Up Short

"Everything's not going to go perfect. You're going to have some losses that you're going to have to bounce back from and some things that are a little unforeseen that you're going to have to deal with."[2]

Super Bowl winning player and coach Tony Dungy

Sensing an upset, the 18,000 fans inside the Value City Arena start to go wild.

Amid the pandemonium, my eyes focus on Josh Hausfeld, the star player for our opponent. Cincinnati's St. Bernard's Roger Bacon leads 66-63. Hausfeld stands on the free throw line to ice the victory. Only seconds remain in the Ohio Division II state championship basketball game. If he makes just one free throw, then the game, our season, and our hope to be named the greatest high school team in the nation for 2002 will be over.

Compounding the unbelievable frustration my players and

I are feeling on the St. Vincent-St. Mary bench is the fact that Hausfeld is at the line because my son Dru III was called for an inexcusable technical foul just moments earlier.

Dru wanted the ball to attempt a game-tying three-pointer. When the ball didn't come his way, he overreacted. The referees rightly called a technical on a move that came from more than a game's worth of frustration. It was a reaction to the pressure we had all been feeling over the course of that crazy year.

If I'm being honest — which is something I plan to be — then I'll admit, even as I stood there hoping that Hausfeld would miss, I had seen this moment coming. Ever since taking over as the head coach of St. Vincent-St. Mary's (STVM) ten months earlier, I had worried that there was no way we could live up to the incredible expectations that had been heaped upon us.

The expectations that came with being two-time defending Ohio Division III champs (we had just recently been moved up to Division II). The expectations of being labeled the best high school team in the nation before the season ever started. The expectations that come when your best player is a lanky seventeen-year-old with once-in-a-generation talent whose name is LeBron James.

As Hausfeld prepares to take his first shot, his teammates on the bench gleefully hook their arms at the elbow — the very definition of a connected team. The energy of impending victory is already coursing through the entire lot of them, the glory already held.

Behind me, my bench tells a much different story. Each player is on his own island of despair, united in a common pose — the lower halves of their faces buried in the fronts of their jerseys to conceal the tears. A courtside TV announcer sums up the scene this way: "A lack of composure down the stretch has hurt STVM."

I feel my dismay like a sack of bricks on my chest. Yes, I had seen this moment coming. And no, I hadn't been able to stop it.

Hausfeld takes a deep breath and shoots the ball. It's pure.

With what feels like the eyes of the basketball world upon us, we've come up short. Bacon wins 71-63.[*] Our failure to win a third straight championship seems to say so much about me as a rookie coach, as a father, and as a man.

FLOP AT THE TOP

The day hadn't started well. Despite being heavy favorites in the game, I had walked into the Value City Arena in Columbus, Ohio, with a thick mess of worry already bubbling up inside of me. I was getting over a nasty flu and had spent a good part of the previous evening sniffling and shivering. Between tissues and mugs of tea, I had also been forced to corner some of my players in the hotel corridor for having the impudence to party late into the night with the cheerleaders, despite knowing exactly what was at stake the next day.

To make matters worse, LeBron woke up that morning with back spasms. We rushed him to Ohio State for electric pulse treatments, which we hoped would help to ease the muscles. But by game time, the spasms were back, so I had to make a decision: *Do I let him play and hope he can work through the pain, or do I sit him and just have him try to stretch and keep the muscles warm, and then see if I can bring him in later in the game?* I chose to play him.

---

[*] See Appendix A for a full box score of the game.

Despite the ominous signs, my team just knew it was going to win — not because they were prepared better or worked harder than their opponents, but because they were already high off a taste of fame.

I had tried to temper their cockiness all season, but a recent *Sports Illustrated* feature had baptized LeBron as "The Chosen One." All the nonstop attention and hoopla had helped them tune me out. They were giddy with the confidence that came with so much attention and so many victories already, not to mention the fact that we had already beaten Roger Bacon 79-70 once that season. The invincibility factor had grown up and around the boys like a stubborn weed, despite this gardener's best efforts.

I didn't walk into the arena that day with the same swagger. It was precisely the pressure of such a game that made me wary of accepting the head coaching job at STVM to begin with. I simply didn't want to mess it up. The team already had two state championships under their belt. Now they had a chance to win three in a row, which would put them in position to win four — something no school had ever done in the state of Ohio. Somehow, it felt like I was walking into a catch-22: if we won the state championship, I figured the credit would go to the boys' previous coach, Keith Dambrot. But if we lost, then I knew the blame would be mine alone.

And that's exactly how it went.

The Ohio media had a field day with our defeat, putting the loss squarely in my lap. "Flop at the Top," said one of the headlines; "Coach Dru Dropped the Ball," quipped another. An article in *The Akron Beacon Journal* split no hairs in its assessment of what went wrong, claiming that the "main difference between this year's STVM and the past two ... was its leader."

Those words leapt off the page and pierced my sense of self

the morning after the game as I stood at our kitchen counter. It's not that I didn't feel responsible. On the contrary, I felt like the captain of a ship that somehow lost course and drove into the bluffs. The hardest part was knowing that unlike most first-year high school coaches, who are free to make (and learn from) their mistakes in total anonymity, my shortcomings were in the national spotlight. Everybody could see and judge. Then there was the fact that my son's technical foul essentially sealed the win for Roger Bacon. *My* son.

FROM FAILURE TO SUCCESS

Dru III was the sole reason I even considered taking on the challenge of coaching boys' basketball to begin with. My intentions were rooted in the simple desire to support my son. But the pressures that came with the team's quick ascension into superstardom somehow started to eclipse the simplicity of my original objective. Like the boys I was coaching, I got caught up with winning and losing.

The night after the game, I lay awake in bed, replaying each possession in my mind's eye. I suffered through every unforced turnover, every wasted possession. Bacon had out-rebounded us 32-18, scored 21 points off our turnovers, and outscored us 16-4 in fast-break points. All night, I kept asking myself a series of fundamental questions: *Was this whole thing a mistake? Am I in over my head? Am I really cut out for this?*

When Dru III came into our kitchen the next morning and saw the slew of critical newspaper articles on the counter and me with my head buried into the palms of my hands, he understood just how badly I felt. I was consumed with the failure of the moment and wasn't able to see the opportunity for growth that lay in front of me.

"Don't worry about it, Dad," he said with pure love in his eyes. "We'll show them next season."

Those words helped yank me out of my own despair. Ultimately, working through that loss helped transform me into a better basketball coach and a better man. Though I may not have seen it at the time, I was forced to call upon some key principles that armed me with the strength to endure the painful aftermath of the defeat. This go-to list can serve everybody as a roadmap for personal evolution. For the rest of the book, we'll dig deeper into these principles. Let's get started.

CHAPTER 2

Decisions Create Environment

"I am convinced that every effort must be made in childhood to teach the young to use their own minds. For one thing is sure: If they don't make up their minds, someone will do it for them."[3]

former first lady Eleanor Roosevelt

After that crushing loss to Roger Bacon, I knew we would have to recommit ourselves both as a team and as individuals. Collectively, our guys would have to decide to stop playing basketball for themselves, for their parents, for their friends, for their fans, or even for their futures. They needed to play for *each other*. Only then could we ultimately regain the championship ... and our integrity.

The core of that team — LeBron, Dru III, and a burly center named Sian Cotton — had been playing together at our local Salvation Army gym on Maple Street since they were ten- and eleven-year-olds. They had grown up playing for an

AAU team I coached. My wife, Carolyn, and I crammed players into our minivan and drove around the Midwest taking on all comers, even venturing as far as Florida for a national tournament.

Off the court, these guys were as close as brothers. LeBron, Willie McGee (who joined the team at age thirteen), and Sian slept over at our house many nights. I can still hear them down in our basement, watching movies, playing video games, and devouring food that Carolyn couldn't seem to make fast enough. (*I'm looking at you*, LeBron!) I'd look down into the rec room to see piles of players in sleeping bags and empty pizza boxes strewn all over the carpet.

They even came up with a nickname for themselves: the "Fab Four," adapted from the University of Michigan's "Fab Five" recruiting class of the early 1990s.

Of course, there are five players on a basketball team, so who was their fab fifth? The answer was a young man named Romeo Travis. Romeo hadn't grown up with the Fab Four. He enrolled at St. Vincent-St. Mary (STVM) long after the others' bond had been forged. Rather than breaking into their clique, Romeo proudly flaunted his independence from it. And rather than inviting him in, Dru III, LeBron, Willie, and Sian poked fun at his stubborn ways, making him feel even more like an outsider.

Romeo was an excellent player. His talent was critical to the team's success. In the championship game, LeBron led us with 32 points, but Romeo was next in the scorebook with 19. Yet as I reviewed our season, I couldn't help but think that the uneasy dynamic between the Fab Four and Romeo stood in the way of our team actually *being* a team.

Making the decision to come together as a team should have been a simple one for those young men. But one of the things I've learned as a coach is that many people believe they are destined to be a *product* of their environment, rather than its *producer*. They have a hard time seeing that their choices are the building blocks of their reality.

Fundamentally, our team would have to grasp principle one: *decisions create environment*.

But let's rewind for a second. If decisions create environments, what creates decisions?

It's our intentions. Our intentions are the "why" in the decisions we make. So the truer and purer our intentions are, the clearer our decisions will be when the time comes to make them. The formula, however, works the other way, too. When our intentions are blurry, our decision-making inevitably becomes compromised.

Sometimes in life we make decisions without really knowing or being connected to our intentions, which leads to outcomes we don't want or understand. By holding this awareness — the power of decisions — every "move" in our life becomes an opportunity to create a new reality.

ROOTS, RAGE, AND RESPONSIBILITY

When I look back at my own map of life choices, I see several that I'm proud of, some I'd like to do over, and others that became cornerstones of who I am today. The ones that led to the best outcomes were the ones rooted in my most authentic and positive intentions.

First on the list of decisions that shaped my life was my choice to accept Jesus Christ as my Lord and Savior.

I grew up in East Liverpool, a small city in Ohio that sits along the Ohio River. In the 19th century, East Liverpool was known as the "Crockery City," thanks to the more than 300 potteries that dotted the city. At one time, East Liverpool manufactured more than half of the china made in the United States. But by the time I was growing up, no more than a handful of the city's potteries were still in production.

My father toiled as a janitor for a bank and a jewelry store. My mother was a "day worker," which meant she was a housekeeper for wealthy white people. Just to make ends meet, sometimes they would both take shifts as waiters at the local country club.

We lived in a small wooden home that sat on a dirt road carved into a steep hill overlooking the Ohio River. We had running water and indoor plumbing, but not much else. Several of my cousins also lived in this small pocket of African-American families in the largely white city. A coal furnace heated our house. When it rained, the old roof sprang dozens of leaks, forcing us to set up buckets all around our home.

Growing up, I wasn't overwhelmed by a sense that we were poor. What we lacked materially, we made up for in a sense of community. And one of the places where the feeling of community was strongest was at church. Our church believed in God. I learned the basic Bible stories and the moral principles that we were taught to keep. But there was little talk of asking Jesus Christ to be our Lord and Savior. Our little church was about membership and community.

In high school, I stayed somewhat involved at church, but you could say I lived life on both ends. I taught Sunday school as a matter of community obligation. Outside of church, however, my life didn't quite jive with the image of a religious teacher.

My real identity as a young man during middle and high school came from sports. Everything I did revolved around athletics. It was the essence of who I was. My *real* church was somewhere out on the football field.

From the hillside where our home sat, you could look down and see exactly half of the town's high school football field. As a child, my friends and I spent many Friday nights sitting on the hillside gazing on the illuminated scene below us. Sometimes we'd be caught up in the action. Other times we'd patiently wait for the action to return to the half of the field that we could actually see.

When I was old enough to play myself, I threw myself into the game. Since our family didn't own a car until I was in eighth grade, I'd often have to walk two miles to football practice.

I was an above-average student, which I attribute to the fact that there was only one school in our area. Both wealthy and poor kids attended. With my healthy competitive spirit, there was no way I was going to let the rich kids in town get better grades than I. They might have some advantages I didn't enjoy, but school was a level playing field where I was determined to show my worth.

Thanks to my efforts on the football field and in the classroom, upon graduation, I did what no one in my family had ever done before: I went to college.

Though getting there was indeed an accomplishment, my university years were wrought with challenges. Some were just part of college life, but others I brought on myself through poor decisions. I started at Ashland College, which was about two hours west of East Liverpool. Ashland wasn't a big school — it probably didn't have many more than 2,000 students. I initially went there to play football. However, when I got to school, I decided not to play, which was not a good decision, because I lost my identity and began experimenting with drugs.

THE TRUTH ABOUT YOUTH

Ashland was a Division III school in a small town. Something about the school and community didn't gel for me. I had the nagging feeling that there were cooler people and bigger parties going on somewhere else. I longed to be at a school with better parties and more people, so I decided to transfer to Ohio University in Athens, Ohio.

The summer after my freshman year, I got a job at Crucible Steel, just up the highway from East Liverpool. All of my high school friends who had not gone to college worked there. My job was to prep steel samples for chemical analysis, which wasn't bad work. After a couple of weeks, I got used to having money in my pocket and nice clothes on my back. When the summer winded up, I decided I would stay at Crucible. *Why spend money to go to college and be broke when I was already making a decent living at Crucible?* I thought.

Thankfully, my mother put her foot down and insisted that college came first.

"You're going to finish this," she said with a no-nonsense finality.

Despite my begrudging, her words became my personal mantra upon arrival at Ohio University.

Four years later, the mill closed down, leaving plenty of those guys jobless and hanging out on the corner in East Liverpool with absolutely nothing to do. *Decisions create environment.* Since I was not yet mature enough to comprehend the truth of that principle, I was fortunate that my mother's decision kept me focused and on track.

"The Decision"

I can't have a chapter about making decisions without mentioning "The Decision." Yes, I'm talking about when LeBron James went on ESPN live to announce where he would sign as a free agent in the summer of 2010.

I don't need to rehash the reaction to "The Decision." It's so infamous that it has its own Wikipedia page. Suffice it to say everyone involved would probably agree that it could have been handled differently. As I remember saying to someone at the time, "It's fine to break up with your girlfriend if you're in a bad relationship. Just don't do it on national TV."

While I've never spoken to LeBron specifically about "The Decision," there are several things I do want to say that got overlooked in the media and public frenzy that ensued. More than anything, by deciding to leave the Cleveland Cavaliers and sign with the Miami Heat, LeBron put himself in a better place to work out his destiny. He made a choice that allowed him to fulfill his life plan. No matter what anyone says, he created an environment that led to four straight NBA finals.

"The Decision" also created an environment for the Boys & Girls Clubs of America to help a greater number of children learn and grow. The nonprofit organization received a donation from LeBron of almost $2.5 million, which came directly from the $6 million in charity revenue that was created from the broadcast of "The Decision." For a nonprofit group that has seen its budget slashed over the years, that was an incredibly impactful donation. This aspect of "The Decision" was quickly overshadowed, but in my view, it should have been celebrated.

On a personal level, it worked out great for LeBron. After

joining the Heat, he got married to his lovely wife, Savannah, and settled into family life.

Of course, LeBron has made a more recent decision. On July 11, 2014, he decided to return to Cleveland. I see this as the correct decision, too. LeBron has grown and matured. He realizes his heart is still in Northeast Ohio. The reaction to his return has been far different from when he left. Fans have welcomed him back with open arms. His relationship with Cavaliers owner Dan Gilbert has been restored, and the region is electric.

Both of these decisions serve as an inspiration for anyone trying to make a tough choice in life. Oftentimes, your decisions are going to be criticized and subjected to scrutiny. But if a decision reflects what's in your heart and points you toward your goals in life, the storm eventually will pass and you'll find yourself in a much better place.

His latest decision also brings things full circle. LeBron's career began in Cleveland and (hopefully) it will end in Cleveland, just like his youth basketball career started for him on Maple Street at the Salvation Army and ended on Maple Street at St. Vincent-St. Mary High School.

When I arrived at Ohio University with its 18,000 students, it gave me the energy and excitement I was craving. But it was also a Division I school, which meant that my football career was effectively over. Despite complaining about how much time football took, it had been a very important part of my life in high school. Sports gave me a sense of purpose and taught me valuable lessons about how to structure my life and be disciplined. Without sports, I began to drift.

I fell in with a group of guys who didn't value school at Ohio U. On most days, we would strut around campus, do the bare minimum to get by in our classes, and spend the rest of the afternoon getting high, playing ball, flirting with girls, or just hanging out. There was no real sense of purpose ... no commitment to anything.

The days when I was determined to prove my worth through academics became a foggy memory. Earning the "respect" of my peers became my motivation. For better or worse, in Black America (and probably beyond), too many young men feel they must earn a reputation by holding their own and acting tough. At Ohio University, I found myself among guys from Cleveland, Cincinnati, Detroit, and Akron who had a swagger and toughness I hadn't learned back in East Liverpool. I used to lie about where I was from, fearing people would respect me less if they knew I came from such a small town. While I thought I was making decisions that would help me fit in, my choices ultimately led me into a downward spiral.

After just one year at Ohio University, I was so burnt out from all the partying and drugs that I decided to take a semester off and clean up with the help of my sister, JoAnne. She was eighteen years older than I and lived in New York City. I had spent every summer with her growing up. Her husband had been ill and passed away that year, so she was glad to have me around. I stayed with her for several months, and to some degree, cleaned up my act. Yes, I was still smoking weed, but the extreme partying tapered off.

Unfortunately, whatever progress I managed to make in New York quickly dissipated when I returned to school in January. Within a matter of days, I slipped right back into my old pattern of poor decision-making. For the next year and half, I pretty much stayed in that rut — slacking hard and getting caught up in a life that had absolutely nothing to do with who I really was.

Looking back on it, the thing I regret most during that period was dating multiple women at the same time. It's one thing not to be true to yourself, but it's another to lie to someone else about your intentions. I was telling these young women whatever I thought would make me seem cool, without any regard for consequence or more important *for their feelings*. I kept behaving this way until a situation really shook me as I was going into my senior year.

BECOMING WHO YOU ARE

My inability to make the right choices concerning the women I dated caused a lot of unnecessary hurt and pain. I felt justified in my actions because all my friends were doing the same thing. However, I began to have stronger feelings for one of the women I was dating. I selfishly refused to let go of any of them, even though it became increasingly hard for me to be involved with all of them. None of them were willing to let me go, even though they knew there were other women. I liked being wanted by them. But it all came crashing down during the summer before my senior year when one of girls told me she was pregnant.

The news jolted me, not just because I wasn't ready to be a father, but because by then I had made a choice to marry Carolyn — the woman who would eventually become my wife. Carolyn pushed me to make some changes and be a better person. This unanticipated pregnancy with another woman felt like twenty giant leaps backward after I'd inched just a few steps forward.

My feelings for Carolyn notwithstanding, I knew I had

to do the right thing, which was to take responsibility for my actions, marry this other girl, and help raise our baby. I now had to share the news with Carolyn, which is another example of the toxic environments our bad decisions can create.

I returned to Ohio University in the fall with my girlfriend. We had decided to get married in Athens. That's when she admitted that she wasn't really pregnant. I experienced a huge wave of relief when I learned that she wouldn't be having our baby. After that wave passed, I knew I had to get my life on the right track.

The morning after I wrecklessly pushed her out of my life, while washing my face in the little trailer I rented, I found myself staring at the reflection in the fogged up mirror. The harder I stared, the less I liked what I saw. I saw a man who behaved without regard for consequence, a man so wrapped up in ego that he had lost sight of almost everything else, a man who lived only for himself. I knew I had to change. I felt that God was showing me who I had become. Almost intuitively, I came right out and asked God to save me because I didn't want to be the person I was looking at.

"Lord," I pleaded, "please come into my life and help me be the person you want me to be."

That was my prayer. It was also the moment that ignited my spiritual journey. This decision to ask for God's help and to remain open to His leading set the tone for what the rest of my life would look like. That doesn't mean I had an overnight transformation, but my life definitely changed.

Now I had to make things right with Carolyn, who had transferred to the University of Pittsburgh in her hometown. I knew I owed her a proper explanation. By this time, she had moved on and was dating someone else. But I made up my mind that if there was even a shred of hope with her, I had to pursue it. I was not going to give up until I felt there was no hope left.

During Thanksgiving break, I went to see her at her parents' home in Pittsburgh. Not only did I have to win her back, but I had to face her parents as well. They knew I had hurt her and were not too happy to see me.

Carolyn was very cautious at first. After making some awkward small talk with her parents, Carolyn and I sat down in their living room. I laid it all out. I was completely honest with her, sharing all the facts. I told her how I had stared in that mirror and was disgusted by what I saw.

Needless to say, she wasn't too pleased by what she heard. I couldn't blame her, no matter how much I felt I had changed. I had messed up terribly. While she let her unhappiness be known, I left her house that evening with hope. I knew I wasn't saying good-bye forever. I still had a chance.

At the end of Thanksgiving break, I returned to the university campus where I spent several days wandering around. I needed a better way to live, a better relationship with the world. I had a friend who was very spiritual, but not in a traditionally religious way. He and I would get into profound philosophical talks late into the night. He gave me spiritual books to read on Buddhism or Hinduism — all kinds of literature from around the world. I enjoyed reading the books and gaining an understanding of how other people comprehended faith. But I eventually realized I was searching for Jesus everywhere *but* in the church.

I had stopped going to church during high school after driving my pastor to a church conference. During the conference, I heard another pastor make a wildly inappropriate comment. Like many teenage boys, my antennae for hypocrisy were already up. So when I heard this comment, it convinced me that church leaders were as sinful as the rest of us. I was generalizing, but that's how I felt.

Despite the disillusionment I had experienced with the church, I was still drawn to the truth of Christianity. I felt the Bible's teachings calling me — even if at times softly — back home. My roundabout journey had led me back to God's Word.

When my relationship with Jesus Christ was rekindled, I had a clearer understanding of sin and fewer expectations of individuals. Until then, I had behaved selfishly and irresponsibly toward others. Once I rededicated myself to Christ, I became more in tune with the concept of *missing the mark*, which is exactly what sin is. Missing the mark doesn't make a person evil, or less than someone else, because spiritual discipleship is an ongoing journey that we all have to take.

At the same time, I had been writing a steady stream of letters to Carolyn, keeping her updated on what was happening in my life and reminding her of how much I wanted her to be part of it. In one of my epic correspondences, I summoned up the courage I might not have been able to muster in person and proposed marriage. Carolyn declined ... at first. Looking back, she probably desired a more intimate and personal proposal. Still, I didn't give up my quest.

Instead, when I finished school, I moved back to East Liverpool, which was only an hour away from Pittsburgh, to be close to her. Once I arrived back home, Carolyn began to soften her stance and agreed to marry me, but on one condition — that we wait until she finished school.

Though that was a perfectly reasonable request on her part — we were very young, and I had made a lot of mistakes — I wouldn't settle for that compromise. I craved real change and was focused on redesigning my life in a positive way. I was beyond ready to get married. So ready, in fact, that I gave Carolyn an ultimatum. I warned that if she was not going to marry me, I was not going to stay in Pittsburgh. My older sister had a job lined up for me in New York, and I was prepared to take it if Carolyn couldn't commit to our future together. (It was a total bluff, because leaving her was the last thing I wanted to do.)

This time, Carolyn's mom saved the day. The same woman who months earlier had been skeptical of me and my intentions stepped in and proved once more that mother knows best.

"When a man is ready to get married, if he doesn't marry you, then he's going to marry someone else," Carolyn's mother advised her.

I guess that did it, because shortly thereafter, we became man and wife.

During our first few years together, we were still getting to know one another, but we were committed to the principle of marriage. We knew there were going to be some ups and downs. For starters, I had just begun a job at ConAgra (the company behind brands like Hunt's tomatoes and Wesson cooking oil), and we had to live with her parents while we saved money. Also, I was still early on in my spiritual quest. Carolyn was raised in the church. Unlike my decisions to sometimes wander outside of it, Carolyn has never wavered — not even to this day.

As challenging as it was, as a couple, we made the *decision* to never run from marriage. That joint decision paved the way for thirty-six years of marriage (and counting) and the birth of four wonderful children — showing us just how much power one decision can truly hold.

After a year of living with Carolyn's parents, we moved into our first apartment. Our life together began to take shape. It was in that apartment that Carolyn became pregnant with our first two children. Five years later, we left Pittsburgh and relocated to Akron, Ohio.

During those five years in Pittsburgh, I was close enough to East Liverpool that I could keep in touch with some of my old friends. I even started playing football again, which helped me reconnect with a piece of my identity I lost during college. I was finally coming back to myself and evolving into the man I was always meant to be. By following my mom's advice and making the decision to stay in college, I not only became the first in my family to graduate, but it also led me to meet and marry the true love of my life.

NO RISK, NO REWARD

My steady job at ConAgra consistently paid the bills, but I wasn't passionate about selling food. Pushing the virtues of sloppy joe mix didn't motivate me to jump out of bed with excitement each morning. When I started to coach basketball part-time, there was a part of me that knew I had found my purpose.

Second to my acceptance of Jesus and marrying Carolyn, perhaps the most important decision of my life — which certainly didn't come easy — was to leave a stable, income-generating job to pursue my true dream of becoming a full-time coach.

Coaching made me feel alive and brought me joy. Sales brought me a paycheck. As I weighed the decision, my first instinct was to stick with the steady job. I had mouths to feed and college to pay for. It wasn't like my family didn't need the money. But I also knew it honored God when I followed the calling He put in my heart. By working at my goal and doing it in a way that glorified Him, I trusted that He'd honor my effort.

Carolyn and I had always believed God was our provider, but the day I left ConAgra, we put that belief to the test. As scary as it was to walk away from job security, I found strength in the realization that I was more creative and resourceful than I had given myself credit for. I wanted to build a business around basketball. That first year, I put together fifty AAU teams. With that income and our savings, God sustained us and helped us thrive. I was joyful. For the first time, I was doing something that was close to my heart.

Eventually, I began organizing travel team basketball tournaments, earning twice as much as I ever made at ConAgra. If I had stayed in the comfort zone of what I call "stuck stability," I would have never been able to achieve my current state in life.

While it is crucial to make wise decisions about your future, you can't be afraid to take chances when you see God moving you in a specific direction. Sometimes you have to sacrifice security and make the tough decision.

Thank God I did follow my dreams. During my first thirteen seasons as a head coach, the Fighting Irish won 252 games, compared to 87 losses. My teams have won eleven district championships, seven regional championships, and three state championships. More important, I've been able to positively influence hundreds of young men's lives — encouraging them to develop their God-given talents and follow their dreams.

When we're young, we have a tendency to get so caught up

with the present moment: *How will this affect me now? How will this impact my life today?*

Those thoughts cause us to make choices that only serve the short term. That's why I like to remind my players: while things can *seem* to work out in the short term, your plan has to extend beyond today or tomorrow. You have to ask, "Where am I going to be three, five, or ten years from now? How am I going to get there?"

I am a firm believer of living in the present moment. While you enjoy the present, you should remember that your decisions decide your future. Every time you make a decision, you are making a personal judgment about your current self, your vision for your future self, and your values. Your decisions are not going to please everyone.

If you seek counsel from your parents (or other trusted adults in your life) and make sure your desires line up with God's Word, then you should be able to make the decision that's best for you. Don't allow "the voices" to take you off God's path. Understanding our intentions leads us on a path of responsible choices — and our choices shape an environment that will give us more options in life.

As my pastor, Bishop Joey Johnson, says: "You have choice. And your choice has impact upon your direction. If you don't use your choice, don't blame God, don't blame the people around you, and don't blame your circumstances. You can always exercise your choice."[4]

BEYOND THE COURT

Question: What decisions have you made that resulted in moving you toward your future goals? Have you made any decisions that negatively impacted your life and went against your true self? Did you turn things around? How?

Question: Have you ever seen hypocrisy in the church? What was your reaction? Were you able to separate Christ's holiness from people's sinful actions? Why or why not?

Question: What's the most important decision you've ever made in your life? How did it help create the environment you're currently living in?

CHAPTER 3

The Power of Words

"A word fitly spoken *is like* apples of gold in settings of silver."

Proverbs 25:11 (NKJV)

I grew up on the idea that your word is your bond. Your actions should line up with what you say. When they do, people respect you more. That's what integrity is about. By sticking with the belief that "actions speak louder than words," I've always been a quiet type of person.

But what I don't say with words, I hope to convey with my actions. People are watching — whether I'm walking the sidelines during a basketball game or out to dinner with my family. You're being looked at all of the time too. In the school hallway or on the athletic field, people want to see if your walk matches your talk. My model in how I conduct myself is Jesus Christ, who always lived out what He said.

HURT AND HEALING

Whether you're quiet like me, or more of a talker, nobody is exempt from feeling the power of words.

During my first year as head coach at St. Vincent-St. Mary, I experienced the highs and lows that words can bring. Losing our final game of the season to Roger Bacon was downright painful, not only because it cost us a third consecutive championship, but also because of everything that led up to the loss.

To understand the atmosphere, think about the swagger that having your image on the cover of *Sports Illustrated* would give you. All of our games sold out. So many people wanted to watch us play that our home games had to be played at a local college instead of at our own gym. Tickets would be resold for hundreds of dollars. Highlights of our players would be viewed thousands of times on the Internet and even by millions on ESPN. The combination of fame and arrogance had created a certain nonchalance that I'd never seen in this group of players.

Of course, I was not free from blame either. Being the coach of such a successful team inevitably changed my approach. I became fixated on winning a championship. Instead of teaching the principles that had drawn me to coaching in the first place, I looked at just X's and O's. Even though I was frustrated about the boys' cockiness and the amount of media attention we received, controlling any of it felt beyond my grasp. If I'm being honest, I surrendered to a certain degree. I stopped fighting and went along for the ride.

That ride came to an abrupt halt when the final buzzer sounded.

The game was over, and my team was in shambles. Willie, who had barely gotten off the bench during the game, was in tears. (A shoulder injury during his freshman year had sidelined Willie's basketball career and severely diminished his role on the team.) Romeo went completely dark, his eyes wild with rage. He looked like he was ready to hit the first person to cross his path. Dru III was sobbing inconsolably. His technical foul had essentially sealed the victory for Roger Bacon, but so many other reasons had factored into our loss. Sian, who refused to wear the second-place silver medallion, tried in vain to calm down Dru. LeBron didn't cry. While he was frustrated, he — more than the others — seemed to accept the defeat. He walked over to the Roger Bacon players and shook all their hands, his expression earnest, but his heart broken.

Despite LeBron's stoicism, the boys' pain was palpable, as was mine. I didn't sleep a wink the night following the game, rehashing its twists and turns in my mind, wondering what I could have done differently. But the real torment kicked in when I woke up the next morning and opened the newspapers. One sportswriter in particular cut the deepest, when he wrote, "When the team needed him most, Coach Dru Joyce let them down."

When I saw those words for the first time, I felt the anger bubbling up inside me. My gut burned. This writer didn't know anything about me or about what I had done for this team over the years. I felt my defenses kicking in like a boxer's. I was ready to pounce. I wanted to send this writer a letter so he would know that I was not only their coach, but also their mentor, their guide, and their number one fan. I felt desperate for him to understand just how much of my time and energy I had given over the course of the years. I needed him to get the fact that my whole purpose in life was to *never let them down*.

That piece of scrutiny, which was just one of many that day, tore through me like claws. I was wounded. I knew the boys had wanted to win four consecutive state championships.

Now, that dream would never become a reality. The loss of that dream hurt, but adding to the pain was the smearing words of journalists who seemed to almost celebrate our defeat.

But just as words can hurt, they can also heal.

After reading the articles, I slumped on our kitchen counter in grief, the local sports sections fanned out in front of me like a collage of bad news. My head hung low. My mind spun with doubt and regret. I was bleary-eyed from lack of sleep. I didn't know how to face the day, much less myself.

I heard my son's footsteps behind me. I shook my head, still unable to come to terms with having to face anyone, much less Dru, whose eyes I was afraid to meet. I was not prepared to have that talk. I had no words for him.

Fortunately, I didn't have to.

In that moment, *his* words saved me. He came over cautiously, looking at the strewn out newspapers. Neither of us had anything to say about the headlines and how much they hurt.

"Don't worry about it, Dad," he finally said, each word cool and calming like a drop of aloe on a nasty cut. "We're going to show them next season."

But the pain was still too raw, and so was I.

"I'm going to write this reporter a letter," I said, feeling the bitterness inside me. "Who does he think he is?"

"Dad, leave it," Dru replied. "Don't waste your time writing that guy a single word. Let's just show him instead."

My wise young son looked at me with his trademark determination. I looked around for the first time and noticed that my wife was also standing in the kitchen. I suddenly felt warm and safe again.

"Dru's right," Carolyn said. "Besides, journalists love to feed off other people's hardships. That's their problem. Let's go out there and show everyone who you really are."

Her potent, healing words warmed my soul. In that instant, I remembered a passage from Proverbs 12:18 that says: "The words of the reckless pierce like swords, but the tongue of the wise brings healing."

Just as the biting words of the media slashed into me that awful morning, my family's supportive words sewed me back up. And it hit me that "what goes up must come down," but the opposite is also true. With the support and encouragement that came in the form of my loved ones' words, I was ready to climb again.

WATCH YOUR WORDS

Since basketball *is* my vehicle, let's use an analogy. Think of each and every word that comes out of your mouth like a crucial play in a high-pressure game. Every utterance has the power to dictate what happens next.

A word packed with positive energy can lead to more good things. You can "get on a roll" with your words and build a healthy lead in life. Just the opposite is true as well. I've had players who sulked on the bench because of their lack of playing time. When I did put them in the game, they played with a sulky attitude. Our words do the same thing. Negativity leads to more negativity. Through sarcasm and crassness, you can dig a deep hole in relationships.

Sometimes we just throw out words mindlessly, but even those words are *loaded* with meaning to the people who hear them. Words hold the power to be both malicious and medicinal. Every word spoken carries with it the potential to cause good or bad. Time and again, I've seen how careless words defeat and how positive words lead to victory.

Words to Live By

At some point, I remember reading about a Christian coach at a Division II school somewhere in Oregon. He ran his program according to seven principles, words really, that we ended up adopting at St. Vincent-St. Mary.

- Unity
- Discipline
- Thankfulness
- Servanthood
- Passion
- Integrity
- Humility

On many occasions, we taped these words on the walls of our locker room. The last thing the boys saw before making their entrance onto a court were these words — words that lead to true success.

Tape these words on your bathroom mirror or above your door as a reminder of the best way to live.

Before each game, I pray with my team. I speak words out loud to acknowledge God. I also want my players to focus their thoughts on the task before us. When we articulate our requests to God, we make our thoughts known to the people around us. Then they can see, along with us, how God answers.

But let's go even farther back to look at the power of words. The Bible says that God created the world through ten utterances of speech. He willed creation into existence just by *saying so*. Think about that for a minute. Now that's power!

Stick with Scripture for a moment and check out what the apostle Paul wrote in Ephesians 4:29, "Do not let any unwholesome talk come out of your mouths, but only what is helpful for building others up according to their needs, that it may benefit those who listen." Unwholesome talk covers a lot of ground. It could mean crude joking, gossiping about others, spreading rumors, and a host of other negative ways to use words.

Now, look at how Paul says we *should* use our words — to build up and benefit the people around us.

Researchers have studied the power of words in our lives. The results of negative words can last for years. They can sit and fester. They can, however, be overcome. Studies show that it takes five positive comments to overcome the power of one negative blast.[5] Negative words hurt, but they can be defeated.

King Solomon has been called one of the wisest leaders who ever lived. In Proverbs 16:24, he tells us, "Gracious words are like a honeycomb, sweet to the soul and healing to the bones." Countless examples come up throughout the Bible where the proper use of words is encouraged. Whether you believe in these teachings or not, it's hard to ignore how often and how seriously words are taken in God's Word.

The Bible provides guidance for my life and billions of others around the world. I've always been a voracious reader. Books can have a profound, life-changing impact. I tell my players that *readers are leaders*. The power of words isn't limited to the spoken word. What you write also has a lot of weight. Your texts, tweets, and posts on social media should also be done with thoughtfulness, acknowledging the power of the written word.

REAL TALK

Many times we're careful with the words we speak to strangers or the different authority figures in our lives, but an unkind word can slip out around the people we love most. We can underestimate the words we say, especially those said in jest. Sadly, I know the words I said to my daughter Ursula hurt her as she grew up. Even though my intentions were never malicious, the words left a mark on her that I wish I could take back.

My daughter, being in the throes of all the various things young girls face growing up, would sometimes react to situations with what I felt was a bit of extra emotion. In response to her reactions, my wife and I would sometimes jokingly refer to Ursula as a "drama queen." We meant no harm. The last thing we wanted to do was add fuel to the burning fires of preteen angst, but unfortunately, that is exactly what we did.

Thankfully, our family has always felt safe talking to each other. Ursula shared with our other daughter, India, how much those words hurt. India then told my wife how being called a drama queen was painful to Ursula. The label made her feel that we didn't take her seriously. That feeling had lingered even into adulthood, which is when she eventually told her sister about it.

Ursula has grown up to be a wonderful young woman. She has forgiven us for our shortsightedness, but sometimes it's harder to forgive ourselves when our words hurt someone. My thoughtless comments became etched in our daughter's life script, which is something that could have been avoided if Carolyn and I had been more attuned to being impeccable with our speech.

Once I knew how my speech had hurt Ursula, I called

her and apologized for how our words affected her, even into adulthood. I made it clear that our intentions were never to make her feel like we didn't care. We were insensitive. The conversation and my apology healed our relationship in an area where we never knew healing was required — the power of words.

As badly as I felt about hurting my daughter's feelings, I came away from that experience proud that my girls talked about it and confided in one another. Putting up a tough front and acting like words don't hurt doesn't work. It may be difficult, but you have to talk about your feelings to grow into a healthy adult.

Not only do we have to understand that our own words carry a punch, but we have to be careful not to give the words of other people power over us. I missed this when I allowed the words of the media to consume me the morning after the state championship game.

Instead of identifying with the painful words that come our way, we should observe them for what they are — someone else's point of view. The lesson here is to file verbal attacks under "things we can't control." Rather than letting harsh words seep into us, we should allow them to pass in one ear and out the other as they dissipate into thin air.

Finally, it is important to be clear and concise with our words. When we fail to let people know what we expect of them or how we're feeling, it can lead them to make assumptions. Too many times, I've seen the damaging impact of assumptions, so I go out of my way to make sure my players clearly understand my expectations. When they make the team, I express to them the significance of being a part of the STVM tradition. For the parents, I hold a preseason meeting where I stress my expectations of families. I don't want the parents to assume I have an open-door policy where they can come and vent their frustrations about playing time, strategy, or another player. I make it clear that I will only talk to them about their son and his development.

The antidote to assumptions is to speak with clarity. Seek to speak the truth and to use your words to communicate clearly with people you love and interact with.

A coin has two sides, and language is no different. Words can lift up through prayer, gratitude, and compliments. Words can damage through cursing, gossip, and slander. This is why it's so critical to focus on positive words and thoughts. Like Jesus, who knew more about the power of words than anybody who has ever walked the planet, said in Matthew 12:37, "For by your words you will be acquitted, and by your words you will be condemned."

BEYOND THE COURT

Question: How have you seen the power of words in your own life? When have your words caused trouble? What words have you said that had a positive impact?

Question: Read James 3:3 – 10 in the Bible. Why does the tongue have so much power? Why is it so easy for us to bless and curse with the same mouth?

Question: In what ways can you use your speech this week to build up the people around you?

CHAPTER 4

The Myth of the Self-Made Man

"If I have seen further, it is by standing on the shoulders of giants."[6]

scientist Sir Isaac Newton

Oftentimes, the right mentors can make the difference between success and failure — not just in sports, but also in all other aspects of life. No matter what society may tell you, there's no such thing as the self-made man. I'm not saying that those who overcome hardships and discrimination through hard work and determination should not be celebrated. But the fact is you can't always be pulling yourself up by your bootstraps. Bootstraps can break. At the end of the day, we depend on the key people in our lives.

I'm grateful for the powerful and diverse arsenal of mentors who helped shape me while I was growing up, and all the way through to adulthood, and even now. People come into our lives at different times for different reasons. The trick is

51

to know how to identify the ones who are there to teach you something from the ones who are just there to distract you — because no matter how you slice it, people need people ... at every age.

OUR TEACHERS ARE EVERYWHERE

I was fortunate. My very first mentors lived right under my roof — they were my parents. Their hard work, focus on faith, and belief in education took root in my mind at a very young age. I didn't always follow their example as I dealt with and fell into some of the temptations of youth, but they instilled a set of values in me that set the tone for who I would eventually become and what I would believe in.

I meet a lot of students from single-parent homes, or homes with parents who are virtually absent. They often struggle mightily to carve out their own path. Seeing that makes me hold very close to my heart the lessons of fortitude and togetherness I saw in my home.

Our family was an *extended* family. We had the kind of household where the kids spent a lot of time with cousins, aunts, and uncles. My older sister, JoAnne, left home very early on and went to New York to live with one of our aunts. Being eighteen years younger than she, I never dreamed of trying to do such a thing. But JoAnne's courage always impressed me. She was smart and fearless, and I was in complete awe of her.

My sister made a life for herself in New York. She was one of the first people who showed me that change is possible as long as you're willing to take hold of the reins and *make* the change.

From the time I was in first grade all the way to high school, once the school year wrapped up, I'd be sitting on a plane to New York. I spent every summer in St. Albans, Queens with my sister. Many kids lived in that neighborhood, and we all became fast friends. From the moment I hit town, I would fall into a rhythm of playing stick ball, chasing ice cream trucks, hanging out on stoops, and laughing my way through the sizzle of summer. New York was a flurry of education, stimulation, culture, and friendships. Having grown up in a small town on an unpaved road where most of my friends were also my relatives, life in the big city represented possibility.

My family couldn't afford a summer vacation or to send me to camp, but I learned about culture, diversity, and different people through those summers in St. Albans. While being in New York City will expose you to many interesting experiences, St. Albans was home to so much culture. Count Basie, John Coltrane, James Brown, Miles Davis, Ella Fitzgerald, Lena Horne, Joe Louis, Jackie Robinson, Roy Campanella, W.E.B. Du Bois, and Roy Wilkins had all called the neighborhood home before I arrived. And future stars like Al Roker and LL Cool J grew up around the same time I was there.

Walking the streets, you could almost feel the history around you. Knowing that I was walking the same streets that Miles Davis or Jackie Robinson had walked inspired me. My sister, a true mentor, sensed the impact St. Albans was having on me and made sure to expose me to as much as possible. By the end of each summer, I'd go back to East Liverpool loaded with information and genuinely inspired by the world.

You know the saying, "small town, small mind" — to me this represents the idea of people who are not willing to budge outside their comfort zones. They never explore beyond what they know in order to experience the fullness of God's amazing world. Although I appreciated the closeness and comfort of East Liverpool, it was incredibly helpful for me to know that a larger world not only existed, but also was accessible.

That's why I always encourage my players to see as much of the world as possible. If they have an aunt in New York or a cousin in Los Angeles, then I want them to get a taste of that lifestyle. No matter where you live, it can be very easy to get caught up in the rhythms, gossip, and dramas of your immediate surroundings.

One of the main reasons I was willing to go on those long drives as coach of our AAU team, the Shooting Stars, was so Dru III, LeBron, and the rest of the players could experience the country. Sure, staying at a hotel outside of Memphis or in Orlando might not have been the same as visiting St. Albans in the 1960s, but for those kids, it was big. LeBron had never been outside of Akron before. Once those players saw a world outside of Ohio where they could compete and win, it motivated them to work even harder to succeed.

Traveling as a group also served as an opportunity to make every trip count. If we were in Memphis, we made it a point to go to the Martin Luther King, Jr. Memorial at the old Lorraine Hotel. It was important for them to understand that basketball might have gotten them out of Akron, but there was much more to see than just another basketball court. I wanted their lives to be enriched in as many ways as possible.

You don't have to drive or fly across the country to find inspiration. Mentors can appear in small towns, too. A great example was one of my high school football coaches, Larry Fernandez. Few solid African-American role models lived in East Liverpool, where the main industries were pottery, dishware, and steel. Coach Fernandez was a young African American man who had just graduated from college. He coached football, track, *and* was a teacher. I liked everything about the lifestyle he led. He didn't just talk to us about sports — he spoke to us about life. And although neither of us probably knew it at the time, he definitely planted the coaching bug in me.

He leveled with us. He told us it was okay to be young and want to have fun. But he also warned that if we weren't prepared for life, it would chew us up and spit us out. To drive home that message, he pointed out people we knew. These individuals were still joking and treating life like a party, even though now the joke was on them. They might have been good athletes ten or fifteen years beforehand, but now they were just hustling or hanging around the bars of East Liverpool. Clearly, they didn't have a plan to do anything with their lives.

Coach Fernandez would tell us that no matter how great an athlete you happened to be in high school, you must have a big-picture plan that transcends the here and now. High school life ends after four years, so if you don't have a plan, you don't have much of anything.

Coach Larry was an effective mentor because his life served as a blueprint that I could follow. He showed me, by example, how to live a life of integrity and self-worth. The way he carried himself made an impact on me. I want to emulate that for the guys I coach, have coached, and will continue to coach.

THE WIZARD OF WESTWOOD

When I took over coaching the Shooting Stars, I tried not to focus on winning. Instead, I focused on the steps it takes to be a winner — being good teammates, communicating, and cultivating skill as individuals and cohesiveness as a group. We drilled the fundamentals, not only how to dribble and shoot, but how to move around the court when they didn't have the ball, how to stay with their man on defense, and how to box out their man for a rebound. The difference between a good team and a great team is the attention paid to the details. That is true for basketball as much as it is for life. By the time they started playing other teams, my kids' skill levels were well above average for their age.

More so than individual skill (which is to say nothing of the out-of-this-world ability LeBron demonstrated), what I really loved about the Shooting Stars was their bond as a team. Despite the fact that LeBron was clearly the most skilled player on whatever floor he walked, it wasn't just him and some nameless sidekicks. The Shooting Stars were a team.

If I allow myself any credit in helping mold these attributes, then I have to say that the inspiration to preach teamwork and selflessness was something that was mentored to me. And the coach who taught me that was the legendary John Wooden.

LeBron's Mentors

Mentors helped mold LeBron James into the superstar he is today. LeBron has obviously been blessed with incredible physical abilities, but there's no way to overlook that he was shortchanged in other areas. Growing up, Dru III always had me; Sian had his father, Lee; Willie had his older brother. But LeBron always lacked a father figure to latch onto. As a youngster, he and his mother, Gloria, moved around constantly — to the point that sometimes they didn't know if or where they would have a place to lay their heads the next night. Even during periods when they did have a steady place to stay, they often weren't the type of places that you'd want to be. Many nights, LeBron fell asleep to the sounds of loud music, sirens, or gunshots.

Fortunately for him, LeBron had enough positive influences to help turn those awful sounds that once filled his childhood into the sounds of dribbling basketballs and the powerful *swoosh* of his own dunks.

No matter how gifted LeBron has always been, his ultimate strength was fueled by the love and support his friends and teammates provided to him. Even today, when you watch LeBron play in the NBA, it's evident how much love there is between him and his teammates. That might seem like a trite observation. *Well, of course they love him, he's the best player on the team,* you might think. But being the best player on a team doesn't always translate into being beloved. Quite frequently, the opposite is true.

While his mother, his teammates, my wife, and I certainly helped give LeBron a sense of family and stability, other individuals helped build him up as a young man. When he was a fourth-grader, his mother sent LeBron to live with his Pee Wee football coach and his family, the Walkers, until she could get herself back on her feet. They were a disciplined family. LeBron was expected to wake up early and show up for his chores. Just like the rest of the Walker kids, LeBron had to help wash the dishes, sweep the floors, scrub countertops, and take out the trash. The family gave him a dose of stability that laid the groundwork for who he would eventually become.

Ultimately, he found his sense of self on the basketball court. He directed much of his energy toward emulating NBA stars. When his mother found a place for them to live, he transformed his bedroom into a veritable shrine to Michael Jordan, Kobe Bryant, and Allen Iverson. All of them were plastered on his walls like a wallpaper of his future dreams.

Unfortunately, when we look at superstars like LeBron, we tend to think they are self-made. The truth is that to reach the heights LeBron has reached takes a great deal of support, mentorship, and role-modeling. Many people have helped LeBron along his journey — from his mother to our family to the Walkers or the Cottons to his teammates and even to folks like Maverick Carter, who transitioned from a teammate to one of LeBron's closet advisors. LeBron's example is another reason to debunk the myth that real men always go at it alone.

Now to be clear, I never met Coach Wooden, let alone played for him or coached under him. For those of you unfamiliar, Coach Wooden was the longtime head basketball coach at UCLA, where he won eleven NCAA championships. His teams won an amazing eighty-eight games in a row. Coach Wooden stressed the tiniest details — even teaching his players how to properly put on their socks so they wouldn't get blisters.

When he retired in 1975, he went down in history as one of the greatest — if not *the* greatest — basketball coaches of all time. Known as the "Wizard of Westwood," Coach Wooden never really liked the nickname. He was a firm follower of Jesus Christ. Despite all of his victories, he believed, "There is only one kind of life that truly wins, and that is the one that places faith in the hands of the Savior."[7]

Even though I never had the chance to meet him personally, Coach Wooden was a key figure in my development as a coach. When I first started coaching the Shooting Stars, my knowledge of the game wasn't any deeper than that of a casual fan. Sure, I could play the game a little bit myself. And like most fans, I'd act like a know-it-all and complain about a coach's strategy when I watched a game on TV. But when it came time to give these boys technical instruction on my own, it became apparent that I was out of my league — even with eleven-year-olds.

One of the first places I turned for instruction was Coach Wooden's books. I was drawn to him because, like me, he was a Christian. Plus, UCLA was my favorite team growing up. I watched them play every chance I got. So between his faith and his success, Coach Wooden seemed like a great place to start.

I read every single one of his books — soaking up his methodology. I'd always believed that readers are leaders, and I had faith that this immersion into Coach Wooden's approach would not only serve me well, but would also be the best thing for my players.

Much of what he taught has stayed with me over the years, but there was one saying in particular that really left a mark. I wrote it down on a piece of paper and taped it to the dashboard of my car. At the time, I was driving the team to different places for practices and games, so we were on the road a lot. To me, it was important that these words were always front and center. Coach Wooden said: *"Talent is God-given, be thankful; fame is man-given, be humble; conceit is self-given, be careful."*[8]

I came back to this quote again and again with the boys, especially when success flooded our way like a tidal wave. I wanted my boys to grasp the fact that they were part of something bigger than themselves. They had a role to play in their success, but it was a host of other people who made them winners.

Coach Wooden also helped recast my definition of competition. In some ways, people don't see the nature of competition as an innately Christian principle. But as John

Wooden wrote and coached, competition has nothing to do with the other team. Instead it's how a group comes together to work toward a common goal. That's what we focused on as a team. It's not about who you're playing *against* — it's about who you are playing *with*.

Coach Wooden's hyper-focus on the power of collaboration informed so much of the way I coach. He made it clear that for the group to be successful, each individual would have to be willing to sacrifice. "A player who makes the team great is better than a great player,"[9] he wrote. Ultimately, our team's success was based on how we played as a group. I couldn't do it alone, nor could they. Not even LeBron.

When LeBron, Dru III, and the others were seniors at St. Vincent-St. Mary, we were asked to play at the Staples Center, which is the home of the Los Angeles Lakers. For most basketball coaches, that would have been the ultimate thrill, but I had another idea. I usually never make special requests, but in this case, I told the people organizing the game that I wanted to play at the campus of the University of California, Los Angeles, instead. Not too long afterward, I found myself coaching on the same floor that Coach Wooden once patrolled at UCLA. Some of the kids were disappointed that they didn't get to experience the glitz and glamour of playing at the Staples Center, but to me, Pauley Pavilion at UCLA was much more appropriate. The kids might have idolized Kobe Bryant and Shaquille O'Neal, but it was Coach Wooden who had helped teach me (and them) the game.

The lesson here: not everyone has the chance to be in direct contact with a great mentor. The key to experiencing effective and inspiring mentorship, no matter who you are or where you live, is to identify potential mentors in an area you're passionate about. By reading Coach Wooden's books, I felt like I knew him personally. More important, his insights armed me spiritually and practically on my own journey to become the kind of coach (and man) that I wanted to be.

This is a critical lesson for students growing up in difficult circumstances. I can't fault a kid whose mother wasn't around for saying, "I never had any support." Just as I can't fault a kid who grew up without a father for saying, "I never got any leadership." But I can encourage them to understand that there are other ways of feeling that support, or finding that direction.

Yes, you should be able to find that support at home — or at least through your extended family — but unfortunately, too many students can't, which is why you need to remember that you can discover wisdom, guidance, and support in a book. Even though the writer of the book isn't someone in your family, or from your hood, they can still help change your life for the better. For me, the Bible and Coach Wooden's books have helped shape who I am. One of those texts was written more than 2,000 years ago, while the others were written by a white man who grew up on a farm in Indiana and started coaching in the 1930s.

Someone is always out there who can teach us something of value and show us how to make our life's journey a little bit better. Just because you may not have obvious role models physically represented in your life, it doesn't mean you must move through life alone. All kinds of sources can give you advice: the words of artists, authors, business leaders, preachers, coaches, educators, and beyond. Mentorship can come from anyone. There is wisdom everywhere. Be bold enough to seek it.

BIG DECISION, BIG IMPACT

Another coach who helped teach me the game was Keith Dambrot, currently the head coach of the men's basketball team at the University of Akron. I first met Coach Dambrot when Dru III was in seventh grade. By that time, there was already no doubt in Dru's mind that he wanted to be a basketball player. Despite being short for his age, he was incredibly focused on improving as a player. I'd often take him to clinics and camps in the Akron area. Instead of just dropping him off, I'd stick around and watch. Not only could I root for him as a father, but I also was eager to hear and see what other coaches were doing.

We wound up at a camp run by Coach Dambrot. He and Dru quickly forged a wonderful relationship. They bonded over the fact that they were both short and both had an incredible work ethic. Coach Dambrot knew what it was like to be a short guy in a big man's game, and he respected how Dru handled it.

During Dru's eighth-grade year, Coach Dambrot accepted a job coaching at St. Vincent-St. Mary. Today, STVM is known throughout the country as a basketball powerhouse, thanks in large part to the success of the teams we had with LeBron, as well as the success we've been fortunate enough to experience in recent years.

At that time, however, STVM was best known as a football school. Coach Dambrot helped change that perception, building a program around an aggressive and disciplined style of basketball. It suited Dru well. I could tell he wanted to play for Coach Dambrot — who ended up being a mentor for him, as well for me.

But making the decision to follow a mentor can come with

consequences. Because of Dru III's desire to play for Coach Dambrot, all of the boys decided to enroll at STVM. At the time, this development was extremely controversial. And people in Akron continue to talk about it to this day.

Everyone (myself included) assumed the boys would play at Buchtel High School. If you were an inner-city, African American kid who could play ball, Buchtel was where you went. But Dru felt he wouldn't get a fair shot at Buchtel because of his size. He already had a relationship with Coach Dambrot and knew he'd be given a chance. Once Dru made his decision, the rest of the guys followed because they wanted to continue playing together.

To people in the community, the choice to collectively enroll in STVM versus Buchtel was about way more than picking one high school over another. They saw it as a matter of race. Buchtel was an overwhelmingly black public school. STVM was an overwhelming white private Catholic school. So when the "Fab Four" picked STVM, they were immediately called "traitors" and "sellouts" within the African American community. But the boys, of course, were neither. They were simply following their friend, who was following one of his mentors.

You may never be called a "traitor" for following Jesus Christ as your mentor, but in this day and age, it's not a popular choice. Maybe you'll feel like an outsider. You may even be put down and ostracized by your friends. But when you know in your heart that you're doing the right thing and following the path that God wants, no amount of criticism should make you turn back on your beliefs.

That's the way it was for Dru and his friends. They stood tall and stood together. Even though their decision had a negative impact on me, I supported them. I had already been hired as an assistant coach at Buchtel, assuming that's where the boys would attend. So I finished out the season and resigned my position on the staff. Coach Dambrot then graciously offered me a position on his bench.

While the controversy surrounding the kids' decision was at times painful, personally, I was excited by how much I could learn from Coach Dambrot. He had already been a Division I college coach at Central Michigan, so it was invaluable for me to be able to watch him in action.

Dambrot took a more detailed and structured approach to coaching than I had been exposed to. While Coach Wooden gave me support in the areas of integrity and purpose, Coach Dambrot spoke to the practical elements of coaching the game. The trickle-down effect of this mentorship was invaluable.

But the truth is, those boys taught me as much as I, or Coach Dambrot, taught them. The love they shared for the game was grounded in their love of one another. They showed me the power of true camaraderie. By being such a close-knit group, they were one another's mentors, too.

I cherished seeing them become each other's role models, knowing firsthand how negative peer pressure can play out. Peer pressure can go both ways. By hanging out with the wrong kind of people in college, I succumbed to doing things that I knew I shouldn't. But by surrounding yourself with friends who push you to be your best self, you can rise up collectively.

Dru III, LeBron, Sian, and Willie played their hearts out for themselves and their personal goals, but they did it even more so for one another. Despite the onslaught of criticism they encountered for picking STVM, they stuck together like a family. As Sian Cotton so poignantly said, "you play your heart out for your family."[10]

Whenever you think you've accomplished something on your own, in a way, you're fooling yourself. Anyone who has ever been successful at anything has had the help of someone else. That's just the nature of humanity, a gift really.

As a student, you need to remember that once you stop learning, you essentially start dying. Always hold on to the belief that life is a journey with no final destination, which means you can never stop and just kick up your feet. You have to keep moving and growing. One of the best ways to do that is by taking cues from the teachers in your life. Look around and you will see they are everywhere.

BEYOND THE COURT

Question: Who have been the most influential mentors in your life so far? What have they contributed?

Question: What one accomplishment in your life are you most proud of? Think of all the people who supported and helped you achieve that. You may even want to thank them.

Question: What book or books have influenced you the most? Why?

CHAPTER 5

Use the Game, Don't Let the Game Use You

"Be strong in body, clean in mind, lofty in ideals."[11]

inventor of basketball, James Naismith

As much of a miracle as it was to witness LeBron James flourish into his fullest expression of a basketball player, it was just as extraordinary (perhaps even more so) to watch Dru III come into his own as well.

As I write this, Lil' Dru (who isn't so little anymore) is playing professional basketball in Germany. He's the point guard for the EWE Oldenburg Baskets.

Dru, the kid who assumed the coaches and players at Buchtel High School would never give a player his size a chance.

Dru, with the skinny little arms.

Dru, the short kid who used to be called "mascot" and "pixie" by fans of the teams we were playing.

Dru, the barely four-foot-one-inch kid who had a pull-up

bar installed in the doorpost of his bedroom in middle school so he could hang from his arms, hoping to lengthen his body for more height.

Dru, who had to contend with the reality of being compared to players with the size and skill of LeBron.

As different as these two best friends and teammates looked on the court, they had one key trait in common. What was it?

One word: *volition*. They shared the dream of becoming the best possible basketball players they could be, but also the dream of playing professional ball *on their terms*.

"Guys were getting bigger, and I wasn't growing," Dru once told me. "So I had to add something else to my game."

That "something else" was a tremendous outside shot. Dru worked tirelessly to become a skilled marksman from behind the arc. Given just a step, he'd splash down a three-pointer in a defender's face. Dru was determined to actualize his dream by working with his God-given circumstances. Instead of surrendering to the preconceptions of ball players having to be a certain size, he found a way to excel in a manner that made sense for him.

"He wasn't always the biggest, wasn't always the fastest, and he wasn't always the cutest, but man, he was tough as nails,"[12] LeBron once joked about his close friend. And he was right — that little man showed the heart of a warrior on the court, proving to everyone around him that hard work, determination, and keeping your heart fixed on a dream was enough to defy the odds.

FAMILY MATTERS

But size was not the only challenge Dru III faced. The fact that he was my son — the coach's son — was something to contend with. I will never forget driving a bunch of players around Ohio one weekend when I overheard one of them snicker to Dru, "The only reason you're even playing is because your dad is the coach." I felt my skin go hot.

But Dru refused to listen to the doubters. He worked harder than the taller, stronger players, often spending extra hours at the gym taking jump shots and mastering his dribble. Then at home, he'd watch tapes of games and discuss strategy. During his first two years at St. Vincent-St. Mary, Coach Dambrot — not me — made the decision about what team he played on and how much court time he saw.

Dru's achievements, including making the varsity squad as a freshman, were a direct result of his passion for the game and his personal will to master it.

Indeed, my son's determination to use the sport to his advantage ultimately landed him a position on a team in Germany. Even though I know Dru's dream was to play in the NBA, I couldn't be prouder of where he's wound up in his career. He might not be making NBA-caliber money, but he's definitely earning an income three times as high as most people who have been out of college for several years. Not only is he able to support his family comfortably, but he also gets the bonus of experiencing other cultures. His daughter speaks German (he and his wife are still working on it). He lives in a world that he never would have been able to enjoy had he not become determined to use the game on his own terms.

Giant in the Room

The 2000 Ohio Division III state championship pitted STVM against Jamestown's Greeneview. STVM hadn't earned a title since 1984. More than 13,000 fans watched the game at Value City Arena in Columbus. The stakes were high, the pressure immense — especially for a bunch of freshmen.

When Dru III was warming up before the game, I noticed some of the Greeneview fans laughing at him because of his size.

"Hey, have you reached puberty yet?" one of them taunted.

"This is a high school game, number ten. No fifth graders allowed!" another yelled.

It wasn't vicious stuff, but I prayed he didn't hear any of it or if he did that he'd be able to block it out. Several minutes into the game, we were trailing by 3 points when Coach Dambrot decided to bring Dru off the bench.

"Diminutive would be a mild understatement," quipped the announcer as Dru stripped off his sweats and strode onto the court. "He's generously listed as five-foot-two, but I think everyone's under the general consensus that he's closer to four-feet-eleven-inches."

After a couple of possessions, Dru found himself alone behind the three-point line on the left side off the court. The ball swung his way, and he hoisted up a three-pointer with no hesitation.

Swish. Nothing but net.

Moments later, Dru got the ball at the top of the key. Another shot. Another three-pointer.

A few possessions later, LeBron got the ball at the top of the key. Now he was looking for Dru. He fired him a pass, and Dru launched a three.

Bull's-eye!

After the third bucket, it was obvious something special was happening. As much as I wanted to run over and give Dru a hug, I resisted the temptation, lest I somehow alter his rhythm.

As the first half wound down, Dru got the ball in the left corner again. This time, one of Jamestown's big men ran at him, but Dru got the shot off just in time.

Again, nothing but net.

In the second half, Jamestown made a concerted effort to keep Dru under control, sending a man flying at him every time he caught the ball. But it didn't matter. He made another three to start the half, and then another, followed by one more.

We were in control and ended up winning by almost 20 points. Dru was clearly the difference-maker, finishing with 21 points after making 7 for 7 from behind the arc.[*]

The crowd had come out that day to see the young prodigy LeBron James work his unyielding magic (which he did, scoring 25 points). But you can imagine how blown away everyone was when Lil' Dru stole the show. In an instant, the smallest boy on the court became the giant in the room.

After they won, LeBron ran over and squeezed Dru with a sense of love and admiration that said, *I knew you could do it.* Imagine that. You are barely five feet tall, and yet you've just dominated a big-man's game.

From that moment on, everybody understood what we already knew in our home — Dru could play. And he was going to keep playing until somebody told him he couldn't. A moment, I'm proud to say, that still hasn't happened.

---

[*] Go to Appendix A to find the full box score.

When I advise Dru III, I remind him that "the game" is always changing. For him, now the game has to include a big-picture plan — one that serves him, his family, and his future. What happens when the basketball years come to an end (which they inevitably do)? What will he take from it? These questions, and others, have to play into how my son and my players use the game ... otherwise they could simply get used.

Too many athletes have allowed the game to use them. They found out they were recruited only to make money for their college institution. They leave college without a degree and with no job prospects or skills because they were funneled into dead-end majors with no real future. Instead of taking control of their own destinies, they allowed themselves to be used by the sport.

For a lot of younger players, the game has already used them up before they leave high school. Many never reach college because of ineligibility. They don't effectively apply themselves in the classroom, so they are left with few options. I've had to talk to many of my players about the importance of being a student-athlete. I remind them there are only around 4,400 Division I basketball scholarships available for the entire world. But there are tens of thousands of academic scholarships awarded every year by colleges, private individuals, and other institutions and organizations.

SUCCESS BUILT ON THE COURT

I once talked to a guy who was trying to become LeBron's agent. He had primarily dealt with NFL football players and said something that I've always remembered.

"Seventy percent of guys finish their stints in the NFL

and walk away with no money," he said. "Their careers are so short, and we are so short-sighted that we don't even see the built-in problem of the model that we've built."

This is why it's so crucial to understand that when it comes to sports, the moment of opportunity is very small. If you identify an opening, be quick to jump on it.

A great example of someone who put this principle into practice is Maverick Carter. Maverick was a senior when LeBron and Dru III were freshmen. He was a starter on that first state championship team. Even though Maverick left the University of Akron after one year of college basketball, he figured out a way to use the game to elevate his life and the lives of those around him.

Because of his friendship with LeBron at STVM, Maverick was able to build that relationship into a business partnership. Today, he manages LeBron (and other athletes) through his firm LRMR. As the president of LRMR Marketing, Maverick has not only created all sorts of endorsement and media opportunities for LeBron, but has also created relationships with the likes of Warren Buffet, Nike's Phil Knight, rap super-star Jay-Z, and countless other business tycoons and sports stars. In 2010, Inc.com put Maverick on its list of the "30 Most Influential Entrepreneurs Under 30."[13]

Perhaps more important, through LRMR, Maverick has helped many people from Akron get opportunities that they otherwise never would have experienced. Even though the seventeen-year-old Maverick had his heart set on being a pro player, his post athletic career is a textbook example of how to successfully leverage the lessons learned from playing sports into a life of success.

Another great example of a person who used sports instead of being used by them is LeBron's former coach at the Miami

Heat, Erick Spoelstra. Coach Spoelstra played college ball at the University of Portland, where he was a starting point guard for four years. But despite Coach Spoelstra's success at the college level, he didn't get a shot in the NBA.

Instead of giving up on the game, he played in Germany, like Dru. Following a back injury, Coach Spo (as he's called) moved back to the United States, where he earned a job as a video coordinator with the Miami Heat. Being a video coordinator is probably the lowest job there is on an NBA team. It requires long, long hours without much pay. Coach Spo didn't gripe. He threw himself into the job, impressing Pat Riley, who was then the Heat's head coach, with his dedication and work ethic. After a couple of years as video coordinator, Coach Spo was promoted to an assistant coach and scout. Four years later, he became the team's head of scouting. Then in 2008, almost thirteen years after he joined the Heat, Coach Spo was named head coach. After taking over the reins, Coach Spo led the team to four straight NBA finals and established himself as one of the top coaches in the league.

I'm sure as a high school student Erick Spoelstra wanted to be an NBA player. But when it became clear that wasn't going to happen, he didn't give up on the game. He made himself valuable to the Miami Heat organization in any way that he could. He hustled and paid his dues for years and took advantage of every opportunity he could to prove his worth. By the time he was just forty, his hard work and dedication elevated him to one of the most desirable positions in professional sports.

Seeing how my son, Maverick, or even Coach Spo have figured how to elevate their lives through basketball is why I constantly preach, "use the game" to my players. But it can be a challenge to get that message through to them. If I've learned one thing through my years of coaching, it's that very few teenagers have a realistic sense of where their basketball skills are going to take them.

EVERY MOVE COUNTS

I remember one particular young man I coached who almost turned down a college scholarship because he thought a better one might come along. He had an offer on the table from a perfectly good school, but he didn't want to take it because he was convinced (or perhaps someone else had convinced him) that a top program like North Carolina or Duke was going to swoop in at the last minute and offer him a spot. Instead of getting into an argument, I decided to use some bottom-line logic.

"Let's do the math," I said calmly. "There are 340 Division I schools. Each school can give thirteen scholarships. Thirteen times 340 is 4,420 scholarships for the entire world, and *you* have one of them."

By showing him just how significant this accomplishment really was, I wanted him to see how he had *used* basketball to obtain a free education.

"You've done that," I told him. "Let all the other stuff go."

Then, I got brutally honest. Many times, that's the best thing to be with yourself and when you're giving advice to a friend.

"This is it," I said. "There is nobody else coming. If you were a top-100 guy and walked away from this scholarship, there's a chance you might get another offer, but you're not a top-100 guy. You have exceeded everyone's expectations. Jump on this, and jump on it quickly."

I may have hurt this player's feelings in that instant, but

I know for the long haul he was better served. A good coach isn't there to tell a young man or woman what he or she wants to hear, but instead to lift the veils of delusion and encourage big-picture thinking that is based in truth. He took the scholarship, finished school with his degree, and is now playing professionally in Europe.

The Bible tells us, "Wounds from a friend can be trusted, but an enemy multiplies kisses."[14] In other words, sometimes the best thing you can do as a friend is to tell the truth, even if it hurts. I want to be a friend to my players, which means I sometimes deliver hard news. But it's actually more kind to tell the truth in a loving — but firm — way than to give false optimism by sugarcoating reality.

Another player in my AAU program was faced with a similar dilemma. When he started with me as a ninth-grader, he was small and frail, like my sons, Dru and Cameron. But also like my boys, he loved the game and became a talented shooter. By the time he reached his senior year of high school, he had grown to over six feet tall. At first, he was adamant about not wanting to go to Lehigh University, which had already offered him a scholarship. Having played a great summer where a slew of coaches watched him perform, his name started getting a fair amount of buzz. We moved on to a tournament in Las Vegas, where all the colleges came out to watch him. I don't know if it was all the pressure or just a bad day, but he didn't play well at all.

Despite that debacle, Lehigh still had its sights on him. He, on the other hand, was intent on declining the offer. I told his coach to tell him, "Go to Lehigh, and you'll see a world of opportunity that will open up to you." I didn't want to sound preachy, but I'd seen this happen to many players. Once they get to college, they mature and discover opportunities they can't comprehend fully beforehand.

Well, C. J. McCollum, the player I'm talking about, ended up going to Lehigh. Then much to our delight, he not only made all-conference as a freshman, but also was named Patriot League Player of the Year. Lehigh played in the NCAA tournament that year, and he scored 26 points on Kansas. Lehigh may have lost, but C. J. scored 26 points on Kansas! That's nothing to scoff at. His sophomore and junior years at Lehigh were much like his first — Player of the Year honors, First Team All-Conference, and in 2012 he scored 30, leading his team to an upset victory over the Duke Blue Devils in the NCAA Tournament.

C. J. ended up having a fantastic career at Lehigh. He earned Player of the Year honors twice, became the all-time leading scorer in Patriot League history, and even led Lehigh to a 75-70 victory over Duke (that's right, Duke!) in the 2012 NCAA basketball tournament by scoring 30 points. C. J. was the tenth overall pick in the 2013 NBA draft by the Portland Trailblazers. Had he gone somewhere else, none of this may have happened. He wouldn't have been given the unique opportunities that Lehigh provided him.

The examples go on forever. Another guy came into our program at STVM but didn't perform well academically. It's not that he didn't try, but he had a learning disability that required him to put in a lot of extra work. Despite the frustrating times, he got through high school and received the opportunity to play for a junior college in Kansas. From my perspective, this was nothing short of a blessing straight from heaven. His family was the picture of dysfunction, with most of his relatives living a fast life. Getting away could do him some good. Yet only a few weeks after being on campus, he called me and said, "Coach, I can't take it. I don't like any of the people up here, and this place is boring. There's nothing to do, and all I smell is cow manure."

I got so frustrated that I wanted to hang up the phone. *Didn't he understand what an opportunity he was squandering? Didn't he know all that was waiting for him in Akron were the streets?* His basketball talents had given him access to the larger world that his family situation and academic issues would have never otherwise allowed.

Instead of hanging up the phone or laying into him, I swallowed hard and said, "Listen, I know it's country up there. But you'll get used to it. Focus on the game, and don't let the other stuff get you down. It's only two years of your life. Just stick it out."

To his credit, he decided to stay for the first year. During that time, he started to show tremendous growth, both as a student and a ballplayer. But sadly, he didn't go back the second year. He chose the more familiar route and followed in the footsteps of his relatives, ending up in the streets. He failed to realize that opportunities don't stop and wait for you to be ready. They just find someone who is. Had he stayed in school, he would have been able to carve out a sense of legacy — not just for him, but also for his family. A college degree. A good job. A sense of the world beyond the streets. This, to me, is the essence of using the game.

One of the proudest moments I've had as a coach was when LeBron told a reporter: "The number one thing Coach Dru taught us was to use the game of basketball and not let the game of basketball use us. That set us up for life after the game of basketball in a way I cannot explain."[15]

If I teach my players nothing else, it gives me profound joy and satisfaction to know that I am able to relay this truth.

MASTER THE GAME

The concept of "using the game" is not limited to athletics, but applies to all aspects of life. You can't view athletic, academic, or musical success as a final destination. Rather, see it as a vehicle that can take you to even greater heights. Try not to get caught up in day-to-day concerns. Instead, begin to look at life as a "game" that must be approached and played with a strategy for victory.

Of course, every game has its own rules. For me, the rules changed when I went from working at ConAgra to full-time coaching. I knew I had to adhere to the rules to succeed. This meant finding mentors, learning from more experienced coaches, studying the game, and trusting God that I was making the right move. It also meant respecting and accepting things I had no control over, such as the naysayers who doubted my qualifications or the referees whose calls could affect the outcome of a game.

Refs have a difficult job. They make the calls they deem appropriate. My job is not to pass judgment on them, but to keep myself and my players focused on the game. If I get stuck on a bad call, so does my team. At that point, I'm no longer a basketball coach; I'm a wrangler of emotions. I need to stay in my role as coach and show my players that nothing — not even a lousy call from a ref — should stop me from doing my best.

There's no getting around the fact that sports are, by nature, competitive. Even though many youth leagues have stopped keeping score, every player still knows who are the winners and losers. A focus on winning can sometimes subvert the real reason any of us get involved in the "game," which is to grow as individuals, to develop passion through discipline, and to collaborate.

Using the game is about realizing that the game is there to serve as a bridge to even greater things. The moment we get caught up in winning and losing — in the X's and O's — we've allowed ourselves to fall into the trap of being used by the game.

Even though losing the state championship during Dru III's junior year was a painful blow to the team and me, it was also a blessing in disguise. It showed us that we needed to redirect our focus — to stop caring about being number one. I wanted to make sure my players would come back to the court with a feeling of triumph that didn't hinge on wins or losses. I wanted them to feel victorious no matter what, certain that they were using the game to serve their strategy in life.

Every day, every moment, is an opportunity to use the game to your advantage. Part of it is looking closely at your unique situation. Part of it is knowing when to bend or adjust your view of things. But all of it includes tapping into a big-picture worldview. Your decisions shouldn't simply move you to a sense of instant gratification. Instead, your choices need to poise you for winning the game of life.

Don't just be a player — master the game.

BEYOND THE COURT

Question: What opportunities have you been given that you could use to further your goals in life? It may be in the classroom, through a relationship, or on the athletic field.

Question: Our society is one of instant gratification. Why is it important to have a longer view of life?

Question: What "rule of the game" have you learned that has helped you the most in life? If you haven't figured one out, look for it, and use it to master the game.

CHAPTER 6
Discipline Determines Your Destiny

"It is discipline, not desire, which determines your destiny."[16]

Pastor Charles Stanley

When an eleven-year-old LeBron was asked what number he wanted to wear that first year in travel basketball, his response was quick: twenty-three. He wanted to have the same number as Michael Jordan, the basketball legend he aspired to emulate. This decision, along with the multitudes of photographs ripped from *Sports Illustrated* and *ESPN* magazines that covered his bedroom walls, served as reminders to LeBron of his own unflinching desire to one day be that great. Everywhere he turned in his bedroom, he saw images of proven basketball talent that motivated him to keep working.

From a young age, LeBron showed a burning, relentless determination to master the game. But almost intuitively, he knew that his willingness would only be one side of the coin. In order to excel at the level of the great athletes he admired, he would have to tap into a force greater than his own desire. That force is *discipline*. LeBron became not only intent on mastering the art of basketball, but also mastering the art of discipline.

If you deconstruct the word "discipline," you'll find the word "disciple." When I looked up synonyms for that word, one jumped out at me: "devotee." That's exactly what lives at the essence of discipline — an individual who is fiercely *devoted* to his passion and committed to showing up consistently so that his passion can be transformed into a skill.

It seems like a simple enough concept. Yet for some reason, staying devoted to a plan, a person, or a purpose is the missing ingredient in so many people's lives. Even when we see discipline leading to success, we form a negative connotation with the word and try to shy away from it. Discipline sounds hard, and definitely *not* fun. Discipline seems to require rules and edicts — a world where harsh punishments are handed out while the law is upheld.

This, however, is not the definition of discipline that I aim to live by. Recasting the word's meaning brings a truer sense of discipline. To me, having a sense of discipline is about understanding your purpose in life and doing everything in your power to achieve it with an unwavering sense of excellence. When you think about it this way, discipline is not really about rules — it's about standards.

Take LeBron for an example. When I coached him, he approached every aspect of the game — whether a state final or a pre-season practice — as a matter of personal duty. Despite the raw talent that LeBron James has been blessed with (he dunked in a game for the first time in eighth grade[17]), he never took his physical abilities for granted.

Case in point: he missed *one* practice from age ten all the way through the end of high school. That's right, one. This was the same kid who once missed eighty days of class during elementary school. To him, not being present at practice was tantamount to not being committed. I truly believe that if God had not given LeBron the raw gifts that are evident for all to see, he still would have become one of the greatest basketball players of all time — using commitment and unyielding discipline to get there.

A SHOT OF DISCIPLINE

After the Cleveland Cavaliers drafted LeBron and he quickly established himself as one of the greatest players in the NBA, he would still put himself through grueling daily workouts in the off-season. He wanted to show himself and everyone around him that you get back what you give.

His utter dedication may have been one of the reasons why LeBron was exasperated during his first time with the Cavs. He never articulated it, but I believe he felt that he was working harder than everyone else, which can be immensely frustrating for someone with such high standards. When the team had an extended time off, LeBron would be back in the gym bright and early the very first day after taking a weeklong break. Some of his teammates would extend their vacations by another week, sometimes more, before heading back to training camp. He didn't have the patience for that, feeling that every moment not on the court was one less moment that could be used to improve your game.

Conversely, one of the reasons behind his success with the Heat was the fact that he was surrounded by players who held the concept of discipline in similar high regard. Ray Allen has often been cited as being one of the most disciplined players in the NBA. With a jump shot as smooth as his bald head, Ray makes hitting three-pointers look as easy as making a layup. One time, a reporter asked Ray how he refined his God-given talent into being such a great shooter.

"[That's] an insult," Ray replied. "God could care less whether I can shoot a jump shot."[18]

Instead, Ray credited his skill as a shooter to how he approached the game. For every game over his illustrious career, Ray followed the same routine:

- 11:30 a.m. to 1 p.m.: nap
- 2:30: eat a meal of chicken and white rice
- 3:45: arrive at the arena to stretch
- 4:15: shave his head
- 4:30: walk onto the court to practice jump shots.[19]

Even Ray's practice jump shots followed a pattern. First, he would make five shots from five different spots — both corners, both wings, and top of the key. Then he'd follow up with five more shots from different distances — close to the rim, two steps back, mid-range, college three-point range, and pro three-point line. Between those sets, he shot five free throws. In total, he *made* 150 shots before every game. Notice I didn't say *shoot* 150 shots. You don't get any points in basketball for shooting the ball. It has to go through the net. Ray only counted makes, just like the scorekeeper.

For every NBA game, Ray followed the same routine. And here's another key: when he practiced those jump shots, he did so at *game speed*. If you've ever watched NBA players warm up before a contest, you may have noticed that they never move very quickly. Often their layup lines look like a joke. They shoot the ball in a leisurely, unhurried manner — not at all like they do during games.

Ray understood very early in his career that was foolish. What's the point of shooting lackadaisically if that sort of motion would get your shot blocked in a real game? When Ray took his practice shots, his body was bent low, his hands were ready at his sides as he caught the ball, and he sprung into each shot, just like he would in a real game.

The advantage Ray gained from this is obvious. While other players spend their warm-ups practicing shots that don't translate into the actual game, Ray trained his body to shoot with deadly accuracy almost instinctively.

It's not that other players don't know they'll be better by taking game shots in practice — it's just that they aren't disciplined enough to do it. It's exhausting to take 150 jump shots at game speed, especially when you have an NBA game to play in a couple of hours. But Ray's body could handle it. Through disciplined training and diet, he built the endurance he needed to succeed. He watched what he ate. He would ride his bicycle whenever he could. His choices required a ton of discipline, but Ray knew it was worth it.

So when Ray suddenly found himself with the ball with just seconds left at the end of Game Six of the 2013 NBA Finals, he didn't have to *think* about what to do. The Heat were a few ticks of the clock away from losing the championship to San Antonio. The Spurs held a three-games-to-two lead and led 95-92 with less than ten seconds in the game. LeBron tried a three-pointer to tie the game, but missed. Chris Bosh fought for the rebound and found Ray in the corner. In one incredibly fluid motion, Ray used his legs to backpedal to the three-point line and then elevate for a three-pointer that tied the game.

It's been called one of the greatest shots in NBA history. With the weight of the entire season on his shoulders, Ray connected on a shot that sent the game into overtime. The

Heat ended up prevailing in the game and went on to win their second straight NBA championship.

Did Ray make that shot because of his God-given ability? No, that's a cop out. Did the ball go in because he "wanted it more" or because he thrived on taking big shots? No. Ray made that iconic shot because he had practiced it tens of thousands of times. So when it was time to take the big shot with millions of people watching and the Heat's season on the line, he didn't have to think about what to do. He simply used a skill he'd spent thousands of hours practicing and perfecting. That's the power of discipline.

How Would You Spend $86,400?

"What would you do if you had $86,400 credited to your bank account every morning, but couldn't save it or give it away? What would you spend it on?"[20]

That's a question from one of my favorite John Wooden books. I sometimes ask that exact question of my players. Of course, they come up with plenty of things to spend the money on. A new car, a closet full of sneakers, an Xbox, jewelry, you name it. They're never at a loss for how to spend the money, because they don't want to waste a cent.

But then I flip it on them and ask how they spend the 86,400 seconds that God gives them every day. Suddenly, the answers don't come so quickly.

"Remember, it's 86,400 seconds that you can never get back," I tell them. "How are you going to spend them? What are you going to do with them? Later on, will you regret how you spent all that precious time, or will you be proud knowing that you have made the best use of it?"

The point is if you use your time correctly, you can make an investment in your own legacy and make a difference for God.

As a coach, I try to teach my players that *time* is the ultimate currency. It's not to be wasted on video games and certainly not to be taken for granted by just hanging out. Every second matters — in basketball and in life.

If I put a bench player into the game for just thirty seconds, I tell them, "Make those thirty seconds the best ones of your life. Play your hardest for that period of time — no matter how short you think it is. It doesn't matter if we're up 30 points or down 30 points. Play hard every second you're in the game."

If you listen closely, you'll probably hear God telling you the same thing.

My son Dru III is another example of a player who tirelessly used discipline as his personal engine to excel at the game. As a short player in a big-man's game, Dru had no choice but to rely on discipline to step up his skills. When Dru was a little kid, he and I would shoot hoops in our driveway and play one-on-one. Back then, I was a lot bigger than he, so it was hard for him to beat me. But he refused to stop playing until he won a game. Sometimes, we'd be out there for six hours straight — late into the night — and I would have to let him win just to get him to bed.

Dru III was so devoted to his game that he missed Super Bowl Sunday on more than one occasion simply because he didn't want to miss practicing. And remember, we lived in Ohio, which is football country. Missing the Super Bowl simply wasn't something that a young boy would ever consider in our neck of the woods. But Dru did so willingly, in order to improve at basketball. We're talking about a ten-year-old boy, whose level of commitment was that sophisticated. That real.

So when Dru first met LeBron, it was instant chemistry. They were like two peas in a pod, bound by their shared love of the game. Their passion for basketball became the foundation of their friendship, a platform on which they could regularly perform and deliver, each one inspiring and informing the other with a constant sense of evolution.

IT'S A NUMBERS GAME

God-given gifts should not be taken lightly. Whether it's possessing fantastic hand-eye coordination, having perfect pitch when singing, being able to jump, or having a photographic memory, these are blessings and should be treated as such. But there is no getting around the fact that talent is only one side of the coin.

Author Malcolm Gladwell analyzed key components that play into mastery and achievement in any endeavor. He found that one variable connected many successful people: 10,000 hours. By putting in 10,000 hours of practice at anything — be it writing, painting, singing, or playing an instrument or a sport — you can master that skill. Time is the distinguishing factor between those who succeed and those who linger on the sidelines waiting to get in the game.

What does 10,000 hours look like? Well, consider this: if you practice two hours per day, it will take fourteen years to reach 10,000 hours.

"Practice isn't the thing you do once you're good," Gladwell writes. "It's the thing you do that makes you good."[21]

His point is simple: desiring something with your whole heart means absolutely nothing if you don't put in the hours to make your desires a reality.

While putting in the hours LeBron or Ray Allen dedicate to practice is certainly one of the keys to success, even that level of discipline isn't enough. It's also critical to develop the proper level of *motivation*. Without motivation, practice can feel like drudgery.

You must be motivated to achieve mastery. You have to *fall in love* with practicing. One of my favorite Gladwell quotes says, "Hard work is a prison sentence only when it does not have meaning."[22] Once you understand the meaning behind your hard work, even the most difficult task can seem easy. So if you're not compelled by the long-term dreams you've devoted yourself to, then maybe it's time to reevaluate your goals.

TRACING YOUR DREAM

My dream really began when Dru III showed an incredible zeal for basketball. As his dad, I felt compelled to help him walk down that path. He started playing at a local recreational league in Akron. The guy who ran the league only let him play on the condition that I be the coach of his team. All the other teams had already been picked. To create my team, every other team had to give me one player. Of course, the player I got from each team was the weakest one who nobody wanted. We won one out of nine games, but still, something told me that I was doing the right thing.

After one season of coaching Dru's rec team, my job with ConAgra started to demand more of me. I was not able to coach the following season, but I still attended Saturday morning games. One day, among the sea of African American parents, I noticed one lone white face in the stands. This gentleman was furiously taking notes, which I found kind of odd. Following the game, the man came over to Dru and me and said he admired the way Dru played. He asked if Dru would consider trying out for an AAU basketball team.

Dru was delighted, and so was I. But when the man found out Dru was in the fourth grade, he hesitated. He was looking for fifth-graders. I pressed him to give Dru a try. Oftentimes, to get better you have to play against older, tougher competition.

Well, Dru made the team. I wasn't surprised, because I knew he had the skill. This opened up a whole new world of basketball for him … and for me. While the rec league was built around a sense of participation, the AAU league was about competition.

When fall came around, the man who had been coaching Dru's AAU team was offered a teaching position and had to leave. At that point, some of the parents approached me, asking if I would consider taking on the responsibility of coaching. They had seen me help in practice and assumed I'd know what to do. Though I didn't know a lot about basketball, I jumped at the opportunity, because I had always wanted to be a coach.

To become a worthwhile coach, I knew I had to show up to every practice with a plan. Even before the practices, I had to demonstrate to the players that I held a vision grand enough for all of us to share. I also had to show that the road to making this dream come true was paved with milestones, but each milestone was achievable and led to bigger and better things.

The more I invested in coaching, the greater my love for the sport grew. As bored as I felt at my corporate job, I found joy in the details of coaching every day. I started to cherish the little things: the staccato sounds of sneaker squeaks against the linoleum floor, the *thump-thump* of the balls being dribbled, the crisp *swish* of the ball ripping through the net. I didn't even mind mopping the floors, knowing that each cleaning gave the boys a new slate on which to shine. When you're following your dream, even the mundane can bring satisfaction.

Of course, frustrating moments came. No dream can be achieved without its share of obstacles and aggravation. Sometimes, it was a dispute with a player's parents over playing time. Other times, I butted heads with a player about strategy. Then there was the frustration with a referee, or the sinking feeling that I'd been out-maneuvered by another coach. Part of discipline includes sticking things out, knowing that obstacles will always arise, and committing to the idea that quitting is not an option under any circumstance.

The road to actualizing one's dreams is often paved with less than perfect moments — moments that make you stop and ask, "Why on earth do I have to do this right now?"

Not only was I growing in my knowledge of basketball and creative financing, but somewhat unexpectedly, coaching basketball also helped me grow spiritually. The last place I thought I would find myself fostering a closer connection to God was on a basketball court.

But through serving these kids and pointing out life lessons on the court, I was seeing God more in everyday occurrences. I was praying more and feeling more confident that I was at the center of His will. It goes without saying that I wanted these kids to develop masterful basketball IQs, but as I grew closer to God, it was even more important to me that my players developed their own relationships with the Creator.

THE POWER OF GOING TO THE HEART

If you accept the premise that discipline, not desire, determines one's destiny, then you have to ask yourself: *What are the keys to becoming more disciplined?* My experience has taught me that prayer and meditation can keep you focused, which is fundamental in staying committed to a goal.

The best days I have are the ones that begin with meditation. I'm not necessarily referring to the literal idea of meditation that's built into many Eastern teachings. Meditation means different things to different people, but for me, it's really about quieting the mind and focusing on who I am in God.

You know that inner voice? The voice that tells you "you're amazing" one minute and "you're terrible" the next? That voice is almost always *on*. Our brains can sometimes feel like a giant room filled with a million television screens, each one flashing a different thought or emotion at incredible speeds. That can get noisy. Really noisy!

By quieting our bodies and minds, we can gradually turn off those TVs, or at the very least, turn down their volume, so we can instead listen to the still small whispers that come from the only voice that matters ... God's.

I don't have any set way of doing this, except I try to make sure I do it as often as possible — the goal being *every day*. The Bible says when you pray it's good to go into your room, close the door, and pray. I typically do this in my office for about fifteen to thirty minutes, sitting in a comfortable chair.

Sometimes, I take it further by reading a passage from Scripture or some other piece of motivational or inspirational literature, maybe it's a devotional book or biography. Then

I settle into my chair with my eyes closed and take in the essence of the words I have just read.

The main thing I'm trying to accomplish through my prayer life is a deeper relationship with my Lord and Savior. That's the goal of it. This quiet time allows him to speak to me, whether through the words I read from Scripture or through the stillness and silence.

By starting my day with some quiet time, it allows me to stay more focused on the principles that guide my life. The Scriptures talk about "being blown here and there by every wind of teaching" (Ephesians 4:14). These teachings can come from what you hear in music, see in movies, learn in the classroom — even from that voice in your head that tells you you're not good enough. That's why daily meditation is key. It grounds you and keeps you from being blown off track.

The question is: What are you putting into your mind? As a young kid, I remember hearing the term *peace of mind*. I suppose that's what I am really after. In those peaceful moments, there's comfort that I feel in my heart. The heart is the center of my relationship with God — not my mind. I want God to be first-place in my heart.

Sometimes, we try to have this mental sense of who God is. But I believe our relationship with Christ has little to do with a mental revelation. It's not about philosophizing or reasoning. It's about having faith and trusting God in your heart.

ENJOY THE PRESENT

Many different moments have come up in my coaching career where I realized I was making decisions from a place of anxiety. My choices were not based on reason or the greater good of the team. Instead, the fear of failure, especially the dread of losing, filled my heart and tainted my decisions.

God puts specific people in our paths for a reason. Years ago, a friend of mine pointed me to a Scripture that revealed an epic truth. Philippians 4:6 says, "Do not be anxious about anything, but in every situation, by prayer and petition, with thanksgiving, present your requests to God."

Being anxious hurts our decision-making ability. Peacefulness brings clarity. By knowing that God will hear me in *every* situation, it gives me the confidence to be at peace whether we win or lose.

The focus of prayer and meditation also helps me spot the small details to teach my players that often are the difference between being good and excellent.

But probably most important, prayer and meditation have given me the discipline to stay in the present moment. Staying present allows me to correct (but not linger on) past mistakes and helps me see the importance of the journey by not getting caught up in the end goal.

Prayer and meditation are often challenging for people — young and old — to master. For some reason, many of us can understand how significant it is to exercise our bodies, but we tend to lose sight of how crucial it is (perhaps even more so) to work out our faith.

Part of my regimen as a coach includes starting every practice with a prayer. We pray before practices to remind ourselves that we're there for more than just basketball. The prayers focus us on better understanding who God is and how He can use this practice to His glory and our growth. I don't want the prayer to be about winning or even the thought of winning.

I make sure the prayers are always different. Some days,

The original AAU team in 1996

My first travel team at the 11u AAU National Championships in Cocoa Beach

Northeast Ohio Shooting Stars team at the 15u AAU National Championships

Family photo in summer of 2000

Cameron and me at the Luxor Hotel in Las Vegas in July 2000

Thanksgiving 2009 with my daughters India and Ursula

Carolyn and me at the wedding of our close friend's daughter in 2013

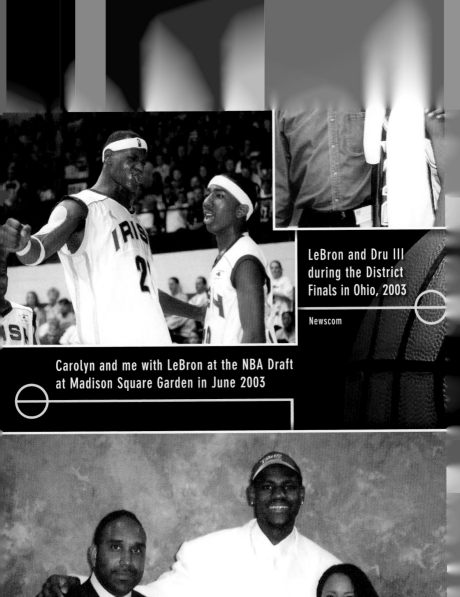

LeBron and Dru III during the District Finals in Ohio, 2003

Newscom

Carolyn and me with LeBron at the NBA Draft at Madison Square Garden in June 2003

At the 2003 NBA Draft with my players

Encouraging the team during a time-out

Time-out during the 2003 State Championship game

James #23

LeBron's uniform number being
retired during a game in 2003

Coaching against our rival
school, Walsh Jesuit, in my first
year as head coach in 2002

Brandon Weems, LeBron, Dru, Sian Cotton, and Corey Jones in their senior year

LeBron, Romeo, Willie, Sian, Marcus Johnson, and Cameron with Dru at his wedding

LeBron and Dru on their graduation day

2009 State
Championship team

2002 preseason fund-raising
event for the Ronald McDonald
House in Akron, Ohio. LeBron and
Dru dribble a basketball for the
last mile of a 5K race.

Akron Beacon Journal

2011 district champions who went on
to win the state championship

The Fab Five and me at the Roundball Classic in Chicago

Our family at Cameron's wedding in July 2014

they are short. Other days, they are a bit longer. Sometimes, I hone in on something that's happened, or a certain person. I don't want to say the same prayer every practice, because eventually my players would stop listening to the message. I want each prayer to feel fresh and relevant to something that's going on.

During the season when our goal was to redeem ourselves from the state championship loss and refocus on our true selves, one of my prayers was: "You have blessed us with this opportunity, and we want to make the most of it — not for our own glory, but for your glory. In Jesus' name, amen."[23]

These sacred moments shouldn't make the team feel that it's part of some mindless routine or rote activity. Instead of trudging through prayer, I want the players to experience a jolt of inspiration. I want them to tap into a sense of gratitude. I want them to see and feel that basketball is really just one small part of their bigger life experience.

Despite St. Vincent-St. Mary being a Catholic school, many of the players don't consider themselves Christ followers, or they simply haven't yet developed their own spiritual practices. I try to treat these opportunities as seedlings that will hopefully one day take root and help the players grow closer to God. Whether you are a churchgoer or don't come from a religious family, designating time each day to this quiet pursuit will open your eyes to the fact that you're part of something greater than just yourself.

You often see professional athletes thanking God on TV after a big game. I have no problem with that at all. If you want to honor and thank God for giving you athletic ability, it shows an understanding about the one who gives great gifts (see James 1:17).

Honoring the forces behind your success is a good thing

that should come naturally. It's not all about *you*. Some athletes are more open or expressive about their faith. NBA hall of famer David Robinson, who won two championships with San Antonio, was very vocal about his faith in Jesus. Other players are more closed and personal. One is not better than the other. Just because I choose not to mention God when the TV cameras are on does not mean I don't have that connection. I just show it in a more private way.

I will say that on some level we need to be able to express our thanks to God — be it in private or public — so that He receives that honor and glory.

My own spiritual journey has shown me time and again how necessary it is to carve out some quiet time on a daily basis. Prayer and meditation give us a mirror into ourselves, which inevitably strengthens our connection to the Creator. People often perceive God as an angry, merciless ruler who is there to punish. I believe that part of my sacred responsibility as a coach is to take the players' understanding of God to another level. By sitting quietly in a world that seldom seems to stop, we can get a better, more accurate view of who we are and how we are meant to fit into God's big picture.

Pausing and praying give us a clearer sense of our unique purpose and help us uncover the steps we need to take to make that happen. I like to think of it as an ongoing dance that you have with the Creator, a harmonious movement between each one of us and God. He gives us the opportunities to make choices in our lives, and it's our job to make the right ones so that we don't step on His toes and mess up the healthy rhythm. The idea is that we are meant to move through life together, following His lead in a constant flow of grace.

Disciplining ourselves takes self-control. The Scriptures talk about disciplining your body like an athlete and training it to do what it should (see 1 Corinthians 9:27). We tend to lose the fact that there is a spiritual battle going on inside each of us. That the question is, "Who's going to win?" Discipline or the easy way out. God or ourselves.

The desires of flesh will always take us down the path of destruction, which is why we need to fiercely cling to our sense of discipline. I like to say we should believe that everything depends on God, but we should work like everything depends on *us*.

Discipline fuels us to stay committed to the task no matter what life throws our way. Discipline is the work that brings our desires into reality. Discipline keeps us in the present moment, without focusing on the results. It takes discipline to be a disciple — of your sport, your music, your schoolwork … and your God.

BEYOND THE COURT

Question: In what area of your life do you show the most discipline? Where could you use a little extra discipline? What steps could you take to improve in that area?

Question: Is practice for you drudgery, or do you see it as a means to an end? How does your attitude affect your effort and commitment level?

Question: Do you currently set aside time each day for prayer and meditation? If not, how could you change your schedule or priorities to make it fit? If you do, what have you seen as the greatest benefit of this time?

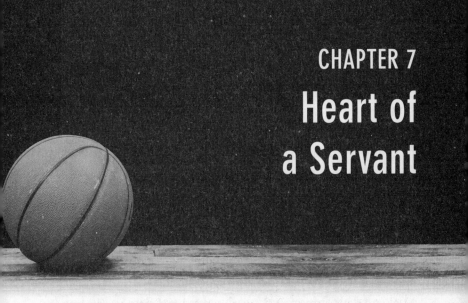

CHAPTER 7
Heart of a Servant

"Life's most persistent and urgent question is:
What are you doing for others?"[24]

Dr. Martin Luther King, Jr.

In elementary school, I loved playing youth football. The running, the thrill of juking a would-be tackler, the sound of crashing pads, and the sense of exhausted satisfaction when the game was over. But looking back on those days, much of what I loved about the game had nothing to do with football. As odd as it sounds, one of the main things that drew me in was the sense of *service* that made every one of our games possible.

Right along with the players running around in grass-stained uniforms, stood the parents. Moms and dads volunteered for our benefit and made a point to give their time so that their kids, *we* kids, could play the game. They sacrificed so that we could *have* something ... so that we could *be* something.

Fathers drove kids to and from practices and served as coaches, motivating and guiding us through each moment of the game. The mothers dutifully worked the concession stands, serving up cold sodas and tasty snacks to the fans on the sidelines.

Knowing what I know now, those adults had busy lives. Plenty of things demanded their time and energy. Yet, there they were, in service to the kids, completely sacrificing their own personal time for the sake of the younger generation. Part of it was a way for them to have a little fun supporting their children. Football was a way to keep us off the streets and out of trouble. But they also probably realized that those weekend days running up and down a dusty field were some of the best times we were ever going to have in East Liverpool. They knew what sort of struggle awaited us not so far down the road, and they wanted us to enjoy life to the fullest while we still could. They gave of themselves for our benefit.

Perhaps I took special notice of these parents because my own were seldom there. As a day worker and a janitor, my mother and father sometimes worked seven days a week — just so we could eat. Their absence made me take notice of the other parents' presence. Seeing these parents and the example my own parents set helped me shape an appreciation of self-sacrifice, which I believe is the essence of having the heart of a servant.

Two words really come to mind when I think about having the heart of a servant. One is *service,* and the other is *selflessness.* And the two go very much hand in hand.

The concept of growing up doesn't just mean getting bigger or older. It means coming out of the delusion that we are on this planet just for ourselves and to meet our own needs. It means realizing that we were put on this earth to actually make a difference. It means stepping farther and farther away from the misconception that we *deserve* things, and more into the idea that we are here to *serve*.

The problem is we're born into this world, and our needs are magically met. If we cry, we get a bottle. If we fall down, we get a bandage. If we're hungry, there's food to eat. Some people never grow beyond expecting someone else to meet their every need. Part of maturity is understanding that we have to take responsibility for ourselves and look for ways to give back.

Think about the adults in your life who serve you — the parent, coach, pastor, mentor, or boss who makes your life a little better and a little easier. I have examples from all of these areas that I draw from when I coach.

SERVE BEFORE DESERVE

When people turn from "taking" and begin "giving," they become more fulfilled and spiritually healthy. Giving back is like a statement to the heavenly Father that says, *Thank you for what you've given me.*

I'll give you an example. When I was the director of our church's youth ministry, we would volunteer with Habitat for Humanity. This amazing Christian housing ministry began in 1976. Founded by Millard and Linda Fuller, Habitat believes that every man, woman, and child should have a safe and affordable place to live. By giving of our time, the kids and I had the chance to build homes from the ground up for families in need.

One of the first times we reported for duty, we arrived at our designated site at the crack of dawn, not quite knowing what to expect. All of us stared at the vacant expanse where the home was to be built. Just the act of gazing upon this emptiness showed us the reality of what it means to *have* a home at all. Instantly, we were all more grateful for our own dwelling places.

At first, we looked around at one another, wondering how this would all come together. We didn't know anything about carpentry, much less about the elaborate engineering elements that go into constructing a home. But the Habitat program had been around long enough that its managers knew exactly what they were doing. They separated us into groups. Each one received a set of instructions, along with the relevant tools and hardware necessary to accomplish our respective tasks. We got hammers, nails, screwdrivers, wood, levels, and saws — all kinds of equipment we needed to do the work. Slowly but surely, we created something together.

The look on the kids' faces meant everything to me. By using their energy for something that had absolutely nothing to do with their own wants and needs, they gained a real taste of sacrifice. Many of the kids (myself included) would have preferred spending that Saturday at the gym playing hoops, running around a football field, or goofing off at a swimming pool. But we gave that time so one day a needy family would have their own home. Despite the hot sun and hard work, it felt incredibly good.

This attitude of service wasn't only shared with kids at church. As a coach, it's crucial that my players understand the value of having the heart of a servant. I need them to see the merits of self-sacrifice — not just because it helps them become better players, but because it compels them to become great individuals.

During the holiday season when Dru III, LeBron, and the others were growing up, a local church would create food baskets for families in need. The labor that went into making these baskets and getting them to the right places was beyond tedious. It took a good amount of time and energy. *Time* and *energy* are the building blocks of servanthood.

The boys and I would help unload tractor-trailers that were full of fifty-pound bags of potatoes and cases of canned goods. We would carry them to the church basement where volunteers sorted them. Do you think a bunch of teenage boys wanted to do this type of labor? We all know the answer to that question. I heard an occasional grumble or wisecrack, but at the end of the day, they were glad they had helped out.

These moments also gave them quality time to bond as a group off the court. Sometimes, we would also get together to serve meals at local homeless shelters, which was always eye opening and humbling, even for the players who weren't in the best circumstances themselves. By serving food to the poor, it helped show that life's struggles are relative. Somehow, we should always help one another, or at least try to.

Just like I encouraged the players to serve as much and as often as they could, my wife and I did our best to help the boys on the team if they needed anything. Be it clothes or books for school, or putting some money on their ID cards for lunch, we did whatever we could.

I tried to help my family and my players see that by sharing these kinds of blessings with others, they were actually creating more blessings for themselves. I'm proud to say both my daughters carry this message in their own lives. My oldest, Ursula, has worked for several nonprofit organizations who serve people trying to get their lives together and people who have suffered head trauma. She's currently starting her own consulting company to help service organizations meet government standards and earn grant money. India started her own nonprofit called *STARS*, Sisters Transforming and Reaching Success, which helps teenage girls. Now my youngest son, Cameron, is beginning his own journey into coaching.

At the end of the day, it's not so much what you do but that you're doing *something* to help others. When I first started participating in service activities, I wasn't always sure I understood their significance. But then I'd come across a player who would return, a little older, looking for a way to help. Now, at least twenty guys have at some point come back and found a way to give back in the community.

THE PROBLEM WITH SELFISHNESS

But there's always a flipside, right? The opposite of self-lessness is not selfishness. It's *entitlement*, which can get a person — or a group of people — into a whole lot of trouble.

As a coach, one of my goals is to teach selfless basketball. It's about the team, not just an individual player. When LeBron started playing on the Shooting Stars travel team, he was like most young kids. He shot the ball most of the time. But I could see he had the vision and ability to make plays. I remember driving him home from practice one evening and telling him that if he shared the basketball, people would always enjoy playing with him. I never had to have that conversation again. He got it.

When your best player creates opportunities for other players, it becomes contagious. As LeBron grew, so too did his excitement about creating shots for other players. I raised both of my sons as pass-first point guards. This selfless style of play has been emphasized with every team I have ever coached.

Of course, it has not always been easy to implement. Many

of today's young players have been trained to have a "me first" mentality. By the time they reach high school, that attitude has been deeply ingrained into their consciousness. While I have not always known the most about X's and O's on the court, God has given me the ability to bring players together to work toward a common goal.

Each year, it becomes more challenging to achieve unity because of the attitude of entitlement. Players come in with a mindset that says "it's all about me," but I want them to leave knowing "it's all about the team." When they're willing to sacrifice for the team, they more easily achieve their individual goals. Getting them to believe this, however, requires some convincing on my part.

At the beginning of STVM's 2010–11 season, our best player transferred, which left a void at the top. He wasn't the team leader, but everyone liked him. With him gone, every player believed he would be the one to save the team. A "me first" attitude developed. Not helping the situation, the core players on the team had grown up as rivals. They really didn't like each other. From the parents all the way down to the players, the team was filled with opposition, selfishness, resentment, anger, and jealousy. You name a negative attitude, and it was there.

I finally recognized that it all stemmed from two players who couldn't get along. I brought them into my office and told them that they were the problem. If they didn't get their relationship fixed, the team would continue to struggle. It was their senior season, and I challenged them to put their petty differences aside and play together. I can't say they had the best relationship, but they mended it enough to make it work for the group. And in the end, we went on to win my third state championship.

USE YOUR SKILL FOR THE GREATER GOOD

Sometimes being a servant means knowing how to identify your individual talents and using your skills to contribute for the greater good.

In 2009, Mike Hammonds entered his senior year at STVM. He came to the Fighting Irish as an unheralded freshman. With hard work and time, he just kept getting better and better. He patiently waited his turn on the bench, gave it his all when he was on the court, and never complained.

Because of the great player he evolved into, all the other kids respected him. As Mike entered his senior year, I wanted him to be the leader of the team. Daylen Harrison *was* our best player. Daylen was quiet. He led by example, but he wasn't the vocal leader this group needed.

From my experience, I knew our team needed a more vocal and charismatic leader. I gently pushed Mike to grow up a bit, knowing it would be good for both him and the team. Every time I pushed, he resisted. Even though he was one of our best players, a lot of times he'd mess around when the occasion called for seriousness. Soon, it became clear he didn't want the burden of being the leader. He was more interested in having fun.

"All the other kids are following you," I told him one afternoon. "Your behavior and attitude have the power to take this team in the right or wrong direction. You're going to play a big role in determining whether we have guys out there messing around or guys focused on making this team better."

It was a heavy load to drop on him, but I sincerely believed he was up to the challenge. He still resisted, so I got a little tougher with him. If he acted up during a workout, instead of letting it slide, I'd throw him out. One time, his mother was at a pre-season open gym. Mike went off on a freshman for no real reason, probably just to get a laugh.

"Mike, you gotta go," I said in a matter-of-fact tone.

It was uncomfortable, but I threw him out with his mother watching. I needed to show him that anything short of being a leader was unacceptable. After the open gym, he came into my office with his mother. We talked at length about how he had treated the freshman player and how much everybody looked up to him. I left that meeting, went home, and told Carolyn that I had found my leader.

The early season practices went great. Daylen was playing well, and Mike was playing exceptionally. Then the wheels fell off.

During a twelve-team scrimmage in Toledo, Mike got off to a rough start. He turned over the ball twice and fouled a jump shooter, which is no-no on my teams. I took him out of the game so he could calm down a little bit. When he came to the bench, I started to say something, but he waved me off. He stormed past me, went to sit down, and started to pull out his jersey.

Now, there are two things my players know never to do to Coach Dru:

1. You don't wave me off.
2. When you're walking off the court, you don't pull out your jersey.

I grabbed his wrist as if to say, "Mike, don't go there."

He turned and cursed at me, telling me to get my hands off him. At that point, I calmly told him he was done not just for the day, but also for the season.

We were in just the second of our four-game scrimmage, so Mike had to sit in the cafeteria for the rest of the day. During a break between our third and fourth games, his mother called, pleading with me to give her son a second chance.

I told her the truth: "Look, none of my players are going to come at me like that and stay on the team."

When I got home that evening and told my wife what happened, she gave me a look.

"Throwing Mike off the team is the easy way out," Carolyn said. "A month ago, you were all excited 'cause you had found your leader. Now you're done with him? Are *you* going to step up or take the easy way out? *You* need to lead by example."

She had made her point. The next day, I called Mike into the office.

"You're not going to win this battle," I told him. "You are going to come back and apologize to the team. Not only are you going to apologize, but you're going to lead this team in the right direction."

We looked one another dead in the eyes. I was presenting him with the opportunity to serve, and I could tell he was finally ready to accept this sacred duty. Just by the look on his face, I could see he understood what real leadership would entail. A leader has the power to color the whole tone and character of a team.

Mike accepted my challenge. He knew that I didn't come after every player like this. I had singled him out because I saw real potential in him. After he apologized to the team and to me, he stepped back in with sheer determination. He wanted to play the best ball *and* become the leader we all knew he could be.

From that point on, whenever there was an issue, he became my go-to guy. If the younger guys needed a pep talk, Mike would amp them up. If someone was arguing, Mike would break it up. He started to see the value of having a player lead the team. And I started to see in him the heart of a servant.

Return of the King

A commitment to servitude was at the heart of LeBron's "return" to Cleveland. The reason there are quotation marks around "return," is because anyone who lives in Akron could tell you LeBron never really left. Yes, he went to Miami for four years. But he remained a part of Northeast Ohio, both emotionally and physically. His LeBron James Family Foundation continued to provide support for children in the area, and he remained a constant — and beloved — presence around Northeast Ohio in the off-season.

After LeBron opted out of his contract with the Miami Heat on July 1, 2014, a lot of people assumed I had some sort of inside information about what his next move was going to be. But honestly, I didn't know. I did, however, suspect that he might come back to the Cavs. I know how much this area means to him. I also knew that giving back to his community would weigh into his decision just as much, if not more so, than what was best for him on the court.

This is what LeBron alluded to when he wrote that his presence could make a real difference in northeast Ohio. Forget about the money his return will bring to the Cleveland area, or even the civic pride the community will feel when the team eventually wins a championship (which I believe it will). LeBron is more than just monster dunks and amazing feats of athleticism. He has the heart of a servant and shows it by giving back to the community through his time, energy, money, and effort.

One day in the middle of January, Mike came into my office and said, "Coach, we're going to win the state championship."

When he said that, I knew we would. And we did — not only because Mike played terrific basketball, but also because he helped shape the direction of the team with his positive and selfless leadership.

It's one thing to have a great coach guiding and mentoring a team. But it's a whole different experience when one of the players can command respect and serve as the compass for the group. A leader like this gives the team a sense of built-in power and a firm direction in its mission.

BE SELFLESS IN YOUR SERVICE

One of my favorite John Wooden expressions is, "It's amazing how much can be accomplished when no one cares who gets the credit."[25] This idea goes right to the core of what it means to have the heart of a servant. When someone is overly concerned with getting the credit or receiving the glory, it's usually an indication that he's only really there to serve *himself*.

Players do this for all kinds of reasons: recognition, popularity, and competitiveness. Some players will play extra hard their senior year just to get a scholarship. But the truth is if you win a state championship *as a team*, you'll ultimately get everything you want individually and more. This is why it's crucial to always put the team first. When you prioritize the team, you're a servant. When you prioritize yourself, the only thing you serve is your own ego.

One of the greatest obstacles I face as a coach is getting players to understand that they have to wait their turn. Many might not play on the varsity team until their sophomore or junior years. Not every player can be a LeBron or Dru III and play four years of varsity basketball.

But our culture is one of instant gratification. Players want the spotlight and fame without putting in the time and service. Players and their parents are eager for the attention that comes from playing at a top-tier high school program. They don't want to hear, "Wait."

In those instances, I say, "Listen, success as a basketball player was not promised to you. You need to work hard and struggle. If you love it and want it that much, you need to sacrifice your time and energy. More than anything, you need to be patient."

Inevitably, younger players want to compare themselves to older kids who get more playing time than they do. At those times, I level with them and say, "It's not that you're not good enough — but you're not *better than*. And if you're not better than the guy in front of you, you're going to have to be patient. Show me that you're willing to wait your turn, for the good of the team, and chances are that I will increase your minutes."

LeBron never had to ask for increased playing time. He earned his minutes on the court. As he progressed from his freshman through his senior seasons, his presence and scoring average naturally increased. As a freshman, LeBron averaged 18 points a game, but during his senior year, he poured in more than 30 every contest.

Can you imagine playing on the team that brought LeBron James into the public eye? We couldn't escape the perception that our winning streak was the result of having him front and center at every game. While our success had a lot to do with the uncanny talent LeBron showed from an early age, the fact is those boys prevailed because they were a cohesive team. LeBron, in fact, would be the first person to tell you that.

I knew I could have favored LeBron, treating him differently than I did his teammates by giving special privileges. Even though he might have liked that (after all, he was a young boy when this all began), I would have eventually lost the support of the team. Instead, I did my best to help my superstar understand that he was part of something bigger than himself. If he valued his teammates over himself by selflessly making them better, he would always be the kind of player everyone would want on their team. And look what happened. Not only did LeBron's points go up from his freshman year, but so did his assists and rebounds.

It was true with LeBron, and it has been true with every player I have seen. When they aim for service over ego, positive things happen. My most successful teams over the years have always been those with players who focused on how they could serve each other, as opposed to how they could excel individually.

Service is about patience and sacrifice, and it's also about attitude. If you come with the right attitude and work hard during *practice*, you *will* get a coach's attention.

Another hint for anyone who finds himself or herself stuck on their team's bench: when you're on the bench, remember that it's not all about you. Cheer for your team. Even if you are consumed with desire to be in the game, guess what? You can be of service to your team right from the bench. The guys on the court feel the energy that comes from the fans, so you better believe they're going to feel it when it's coming from their own teammates on the bench.

If you've got your head down and you're sulking, what does that say to everybody? It's a negative energy that radiates to the players on the court and certainly to your coach. Frankly, if you're going to sit on the bench like some kind of victim, as a coach, I'm going to look for someone else to put in the game.

Selflessness doesn't only show up during practice or on the bench, it appears in games. One of the things I look for is a player who's willing to take a charge. That means if one of your teammates gets beat and his man is heading for an easy dunk, then you slide over and put your body between him and the basket. You'll probably get run over. But if your footwork is fast enough and the referee makes the right call, you'll save your team two points.

Why do I notice charges? Because on a basic level, very few people like to get run over by a player who's flying to the basket. It hurts. It's not glamorous. They don't show charges on SportsCenter. By giving up your body like that, I know you're serious about the team. There's very little ego in taking a charge, but there's plenty of selflessness, which I love to see as a coach.

Selflessness has become the foundation of my approach as a basketball coach. Everyone, from coach to player, needs to operate with the common understanding that we are bound by commitment to each other and fueled by our collective goal.

BEYOND THE COURT

Question: How do you serve the people in different areas of your life? Think about how you serve your family, your friends, and your teammates.

Question: How does serving others make you a stronger team member? Is servanthood a sign of weakness or strength? Read Mark 10:42–45 before you answer.

Question: Who are the people who serve you the most? What can you do to thank them?

"If you're trying to achieve, there will be roadblocks. I've had them; everybody has had them. But obstacles don't have to stop you. If you run into a wall, don't turn around and give up. Figure out how to climb it, go through it, or work around it."[26]

basketball hall of famer Michael Jordan

We all have dreams. We have goals, intentions, and ambition. On the good days, we even have a decent amount of determination to move us in the direction of these objectives. We psych ourselves up, tell ourselves we can do it, and go out there to make our dreams happen. If something gets in our way, we struggle through the challenge. We dig deep. We aim high.

Then, when we least expect it — or when we are least prepared for it — *life* comes out of nowhere and smacks us around, sometimes a little, sometimes a lot. Suddenly, our dream seems unattainable. Like trying to get toothpaste back in the tube, we're left frustrated and feeling hopeless. *Maybe our dream will never work out?*

I've already talked about maximizing opportunities, staying focused, being disciplined, staying true to yourself, having a generous spirit, and humbling yourself. But what happens when you do all of this with lion-like intensity and things still don't work out? What if you have tried every imaginable path to your objective, yet you feel like you're nowhere near it? What's your next move?

Well, that's when you take orders from that proverbial cliché — and you make lemonade.

We've all heard it before: *when life gives you lemons, you make lemonade*. But sometimes those "lemons" can be pretty big and extremely sour. The scenarios range from not making the team, to getting a bad grade, to having an unsightly pimple, to getting fired, to having a girlfriend or boyfriend dump you. And at the harsher end of things, sometimes life's obstacles can be as severe as having your parents divorce or battling an illness, such as cancer.

EVERYTHING CHANGES

To really get at the heart of this principle, let's backtrack and look at a crucial insight, because it pretty much sums up our whole existence. When I was in college studying different religions and eventually coming back to Christianity, I came come across a principle Buddhists call "the universal law of impermanence."

This law states that at every second and even every nanosecond, we are changing — and everything, the entirety of the universe, is also always changing. So not only are our insides changing, shifting, growing, receding, expanding, and collapsing; our realities, the circumstances of our lives, are also always in flux.

Not only do our bodies constantly change, but so do our realities. The circumstances of our lives are always in flux.

One moment, I find myself living in East Liverpool as a single man, just out of college, with no car and zero direction. The next, I am driving my son and ten other boys in a van around Akron to an important tournament. One day, I am detoxing off drugs at my sister's in Queens. The next, I am soaking in the words of my pastor at a Sunday church service.

The only constant in this universe is Jesus Christ. He exists outside the laws of thermodynamics. While everything else changes, He never does. The Bible tells us, "Jesus Christ is the same yesterday and today and forever" (Hebrews 13:8). When we put our faith in God, it helps us be ready for anything, because we have a constant that we can always trust to be there.

In the good times, the work we put in leads us closer to the destination to which we aspire. Someone who is looking to get into a good college, for example, might take a series of Advanced Placement or honors classes. Ultimately, he would apply to a number of colleges and eventually receive an acceptance letter. Someone who's eager to learn Spanish might take Spanish classes and join a Spanish club. Then several years later, she may walk away speaking the language fluently enough to plan a long visit to Spain or Central America.

But for all those sweet moments, we all have our share of the bitter ones too. We run into the proverbial lemons, just for the simple reason that everything changes. So what happens when life brings changes that are not positive, or even worse, that feel terrible?

As I see it, you have only one choice: find a way to *make* them positive.

INGREDIENTS FOR LEMONADE

Turning a bad situation into something good is the essence of making lemonade. Unfortunately, it's never as simple as adding a few teaspoons of sugar to water and lemon juice. We often get so wrapped up in the disappointment of not getting what we want that we're almost blinded from any sense of optimism. The truth is that four ingredients can turn even the bitterest drink into something sweet and refreshing. They are:

1. Acceptance
2. Attitude
3. Effort
4. Creativity

Acceptance is the number one ingredient, because if we cannot accept the things we cannot control, we will forever wallow in dissatisfaction. We have to be willing to accept whatever situation life throws at us. In this mindset of calm understanding, we can truly begin to see other options.

Like all young Christians, I was taught the story of Job in Sunday school. Job's story, maybe more than any other in the Bible, is a study in the power of acceptance. No matter what sort of calamity came his way — disease, poverty, even the death of his children — Job never questioned God's plan for him. He held onto his faith and refused to turn away from God. As he told his wife in Job 2:10, "Shall we accept good from God, and not trouble?"

A less dramatic, yet still instructive, meditation on the power of acceptance can also be found when Jesus says,

"Therefore I tell you, do not worry about your life, what you will eat or drink; or about your body, what you will wear. Is not life more than food, and the body more than clothes? Look at the birds of the air; they do not sow or reap or store away in barns, and yet your heavenly Father feeds them. Are you not much more valuable than they? Can any one of you by worrying add a single hour to your life?" (Matthew 6:25 – 27).

Although I've had my moments of anxiety, my journey is definitely a testimony to the power of acceptance. For many years, I accepted the reality of working for ConAgra, despite the fact that I truly didn't want to be there. Now you might say that taking home a good paycheck for steady work isn't exactly in the same league as the trials Job underwent. And you're right. I won't argue that. But as anyone who has been through it can attest, having an unfulfilling and uninspiring job can produce plenty of anxiety.

For me, it was the question of putting my effort into the type of work that God truly had planned for me. So while I always dreamed of something different, I accepted my job. In time, God revealed his ultimate plan for me, and I transitioned into my current calling. But that might never have happened if I had quit my job too soon or didn't work hard while I was at ConAgra.

Attitude is another crucial ingredient. Having a positive attitude can give you the energy to strategize your way out of a bad situation. By staying positive, you'll be better able to see the possibilities.

This is another principle deeply rooted in Christian faith. One of the most widely known passages in the Bible is when Jesus says to his disciples, "O you of little faith" (Matthew 8:26, NKJV). Essentially, Jesus is telling them to change their attitude. He and his disciples had been riding in a boat on the

Sea of Galilee. The wind was howling and waves were crashing over the sides. The disciples were having a hard time staying positive. They were convinced the boat was going to sink.

Jesus wasn't concerned. In fact, He was sleeping during the storm. When the disciples woke Him up, He reminded them that having true faith means believing that even the stormiest seas will eventually calm down. God has the power to calm any storm. Then Jesus proved it by telling the winds to die down and the waves to subside.

Along with acceptance and a positive attitude, another ingredient you'll need to make lemonade is effort. Discipline and effort basically go hand in hand. Think of discipline as the practice of something and effort as the personal dose of power that you bring to the task. How much of yourself, your time, and your focus are you willing to give to something in order to exert the change you'd like to see? Effort is your gasoline.

Last but not least, you have to be creative. This means seeing past your own preconceptions of "how things should be" and envisioning a whole new reality. This gives you a new target to set your eyes on, with a new world of options to explore. It may require you to step outside your comfort zone. But when you think creatively about how to solve a problem or move forward after a tragedy, you may see possibilities you never would have previously imagined.

UNIMAGINABLE LOSS

Let me give you an example of how LeBron, Dru III, and the others made lemonade. When the boys started as freshmen at St. Vincent-St. Mary, they were under the fierce and seasoned tutelage of Coach Keith Dambrot.

Coach Dambrot had just come off a short stint as head

coach at Central Michigan University, a Division I school. He brought an intensity that the boys were not used to. Even though I prided myself on being a good coach, I didn't have the experience Keith brought to the table, and he wasn't shy about showing the boys that he meant business.

Coach Dambrot's fiery nature was both a gift and a curse. No doubt it brought out the best in his players. The boys hated his practices at first, but once we all got used to Keith's brash style, we saw what was really there: an uncompromising, experienced coach who wanted only good things for the team and its players.

For two seasons, the boys skyrocketed. Dru III saw Coach Dambrot as a true mentor. LeBron, with whom Coach Dambrot was particularly hard, started to understand the value of his demanding nature. Through Keith's guidance and tough love, the team won two straight state championships. They had ascended to the top. By the time they got to their junior year, they were unstoppable — and Keith was the one who had set the tone for their dominance.

As the beginning of their junior season grew closer, the buzz around the team wasn't about winning just another state championship, but the national championship as well. On the eve of the season, the unimaginable happened — Coach Dambrot told us he wasn't coming back.

After all the hard work of two seasons where they'd earned a 53-1 record and climbed up the national rankings, Keith decided to take an assistant coaching job at the University of Akron. To say that the boys were devastated would be an understatement.

Some of the players remember finding out this news from a reporter, though Keith maintains he told them himself. LeBron said he didn't want to speak to or see Keith ever again — he even resorted to calling him "Mr. Dambrot" instead of "Coach Dambrot." Sian was extremely bitter and suggested that Coach Dambrot used them to get back to college coaching, claiming indignantly that Dambrot "sold us up the river."[27] Dru felt straight up lied to, since he basically made his decision to attend STVM on the basis that Coach Dambrot would be there the whole time. Romeo felt betrayed, because when he came to STVM, he thought Dambrot would be there to help him reach his fullest potential.

I, too, was shocked. The day I found out, my wife and I were together when a writer from Cleveland's *The Plain Dealer* called and told me the news.

Later that night, Keith called me directly and explained what I already knew. Following the Central Michigan debacle, this was his chance to get back into college coaching. He also told me about some of his concerns, which had a lot to do with all the hype buzzing around LeBron. Having already been through a media circus when he was dismissed from Central Michigan, he didn't want to be under the same type of spotlight that coaching LeBron was sure to bring.

At first, my instinct was to try to convince him that it was a terrible idea. These guys needed him. The team was on a roll. I knew how much he wanted to get back to the Division I ranks, but I felt like the timing wasn't right.

Then he said something that I didn't see coming.

"I want you to take over."

Keith explained that he'd already had discussions with the board at STVM and promised to support me throughout the transition.

"Those are your kids," he said. "You were the one who brought them to me."

Even though I was speechless at first, I knew deep down

that he was right. Those boys were a part of my journey, and me theirs. Despite having entertained the dream of being a high school coach for a long time, I didn't say yes right away.

As Keith filled me with promises of guidance and support, a world of doubt swam around my mind. First and foremost, I didn't think I had enough experience. How could I come close to matching what Coach Dambrot brought to the bench? He'd held three college head coaching gigs before coming to STVM. I'd been the head coach of an AAU team.

Weighing even heavier on my mind was the fact that our upcoming schedule was much stronger than any we'd ever faced. We were slated to play against four teams that were in the top twenty-five nationwide. Plus, STVM was moving up from Division III to Division II in Ohio. That meant we'd be playing bigger, tougher schools. I knew how tough the schedule was going to be, because I'd worked with Keith to set it up!

Then there were the pressures. Not only did the team and coaching staff have high goals, but the fan's expectations for us that year also were sky-high. Anything short of playing for a national championship was going to be considered a failure.

I also worried that the boys might be too comfortable with me. As they say, familiarity breeds contempt. We were definitely familiar with each other after seven years of long car trips and countless summer tournaments. We had each other's backs, but I also considered that this familiarity might somehow backfire. The doubts were everywhere. I felt lost.

Again, it was the words of my wife that helped me understand a bigger picture.

"Dru," she said. "How could you say no?"

Carolyn made me understand that despite all the fears, this opportunity was God's doing. He was honoring me for all those years I put in with this team. She reminded me of all the AAU practices, the selling duct tape door to door, the sleepovers Dru III had with the other guys in our basement. She reminded me of the principles of life I shared with the boys — principles on which I never wavered. She made me see that this moment was part of my sacred responsibility. As bitter a taste as Coach Dambrot's departure had left in the boys' mouths, Carolyn made me realize that this moment was a way to make lemonade out of it.

So rather than focus on my fears, I embraced the opportunity. With Keith gone, I would step in and do the thing that I had been preparing for during all of those years.

When I finally got my head around what that could mean and began to think creatively, the lemons didn't seem so bad after all. Sure, the team was hurt. The players felt dissed because they didn't see Keith's departure coming. But when they saw me stepping into the head coach role — the guy who was there from the beginning — there was a sense among all of us that everything happens for a reason.

I'm not saying the transition was easy, but it's the best we could have done with the circumstances. So we had to:

1. Accept the fact that Coach Dambrot was out.
2. Consciously shift our attitudes from negative to positive, despite our dismay and discomfort with this new reality.
3. Commit to giving our best effort no matter what.
4. Get creative and resourceful about how we were going to prevail.

Had we left out any of those steps, we wouldn't have been able to plow forward with strength and focus.

RISING ABOVE INJUSTICE

As difficult as it was dealing with Coach Dambrot's departure, the biggest barrel of lemons was yet to come. During the boys' senior year, a jersey "scandal" around LeBron made national news and threatened to derail our season.

For those of you who might not have heard of it, on January 25, 2003, LeBron visited a clothing store called Next. It was located in a swanky Cleveland suburb, and everybody there recognized the rising star. A store associate offered him two jerseys as gifts. One was of former Baltimore Bullets (now the Washington Wizards) basketball star, Wes Unseld, and the other a Gale Sayers football jersey from the Chicago Bears.

The folks at the store not only *gave* those jerseys to LeBron, but also asked him to pose for photos — neither of which LeBron particularly wanted or asked for. By now he was used to being in the public eye, and he typically erred on the side of politeness. So he did what they asked and posed for the shots. He was flattered by the gifts, but that was pretty much where he left the whole thing.

Until five days later when a story with the photos ran in *The Plain Dealer.*

An investigation by the Ohio High School Athletic Association (OHSAA) was immediately launched. Within days, it was decided that LeBron had violated the Association's amateurism bylaws by "capitalizing on his athletic fame by receiving gifts." The jerseys had a value of nearly $800. The maximum dollar amount for acceptable gifts according to the association was $100. The penalty for this violation? LeBron was declared ineligible for the rest of the season.

Can you imagine that? Not a warning. Not a letter of

admonishment. Not being asked to return the goods and apologize. LeBron literally lived and breathed basketball. Now he was told he couldn't play. Here was a kid who made the city of Akron relevant to the outside world. News crews and national news outlets had begun flocking to our games. The whole thing felt just plain wrong.

When LeBron first got wind of the suspension, his immediate reaction was not "Poor me, I can't play" or "Oh no, this is going to ruin my year." Instead, he felt like he had let down his fellow players. Right away, he thought of his teammates. Even though it was his mess and the spotlight was on him, he didn't think of himself. He knew the Fab Five had gone into the season dreaming of winning a national championship, and he felt responsible for that dream seeming to leave their grasp.

There was nothing we could do. The media jumped on the story. Headlines ran across the nation and on the Internet of LeBron's alleged indiscretion. LeBron had to work hard to ignore the media firestorm.

But instead of hiding or shrinking away, LeBron felt that if he personally appealed to the athletic association, it would understand that he didn't mean to break any rules. He was sure that if he was candid, apologetic, and respectful, the association would ease up and allow him to play. But it didn't. The suspension still stood.

Through the course of this incident, I saw actual tears in LeBron's eyes. It was one of the few times I ever witnessed him crying. He wasn't crying for himself alone — he was crying for the whole group. I was infuriated over the injustice of the whole thing, and I knew I had to do something to help him through it.

"If this is the worst that happens in your life, you will have lived a pretty good life," I told him. No one had died. He hadn't blown out a knee or an Achilles tendon, which would put his future in jeopardy. We hadn't even lost a game yet. By stepping back and putting the whole thing in perspective, it helped him understand that in the grand scheme of things, there could be a lot worse problems.

I didn't want to belittle his pain and disappointment. That's the last thing you want to do when a friend or loved one is going through a difficult time. I was just hoping to expand his point of view. I also promised LeBron that I would do everything humanly possible to prepare the team to play the best basketball possible without him on the court.

But LeBron wasn't the only one who needed comfort. His teammates were beyond crushed as well. They felt attacked by the OHSAA and its commissioner, Clair Muscaro. He became the villain behind what they felt was a ridiculous ruling. To them, the association was out to get them.

Where'd the Wheels Come From?

Before the sports jerseys, there was Hummergate.

In December 2002, LeBron James rolled up to school driving a brand-new $50,000 Hummer H2. Outfitted with three TVs and video game hookups,[28] it was the kind of car that most kids, let alone those who live in government housing, can't afford to drive. To say that it drew *some* attention would be an understatement.

LeBron couldn't blow his nose without drawing attention. The shiny Hummer made people around the country wonder if LeBron had taken money from an agent or a shoe company. By this point, everybody knew Nike and Adidas both wanted him to endorse their brands and that he'd be the number one pick in the NBA draft. But accepting money or gifts could ruin his high school eligibility.

Then the truth came out. His mom had received a loan from a dealership in Columbus, Ohio, to buy her son the car for his eighteenth birthday. With the help of lawyer Frederick Nance, Gloria proved to the OHSAA that she had purchased the vehicle herself. On January 28, 2003, it was ruled that LeBron's mother's purchase was not a violation of the OHSAA code.

When the ruling came out, one reporter quipped, "LeBron doesn't have anything more to worry about with his new sports utility vehicle except filling it with gas."[29]

If only he was right. The Hummergate distraction lasted more than a month, and the team had to overcome plenty of other obstacles.

I was a little more sympathetic. I understood the association was getting all kinds of complaints about STVM's unparalleled superstardom. The commissioner probably felt he had to crack down on us to show he wasn't playing favorites.

The truth is that people had a hard time wrapping their heads around the idea that LeBron was becoming a national icon. Today, we can understand why — he truly is a once-in-a-generation talent and personality. But at the time, it seemed like too much too soon. The media said he was prematurely capitalizing on his name. It questioned if he deserved the hype (never mind that it was the media who fueled it in the first place). As one journalist said, the LeBron phenomenon was "something that the system in high school was not designed to handle at that point in time."[30]

One of the worst parts about the whole ordeal was that

STVM itself didn't back up LeBron, despite the fact that he had essentially made the school a household name across the country. We couldn't believe that, after all the sacrifices these boys made when they decided to attend STVM (instead of Buchtel) and after how hard they played, the school didn't seem prepared to go to war for LeBron.

LeBron was allowed to come to practices just to watch. We could all plainly see the tears he would try to hide. In the media and on streets, the talk was only about how LeBron's suspension was going to destroy our season. Everybody had the same foregone conclusion: the team couldn't win without LeBron.

PLAYING WITHOUT LEBRON

The talk was hard to ignore. Dru, being the fighter he is, along with the rest of the boys, was intent on showing everyone how wrong that conclusion was. After all, when you're in a heated game of chess, you don't abandon the game because your queen gets taken. We had lost our most powerful piece, but we were going to play the game until the end.

We were more than one man. We were a *team*. We still had "rooks" that could fly down the court. Our "knights" could trap opposing players and make things tricky. Even our "pawns" had a role on the team. We wanted to win, not only for ourselves, but also for LeBron.

The first game without LeBron was against the Bulldogs of McKinley High School from nearby Canton. No school had been to more Final Fours in the state of Ohio than McKinley. With its strong athletic tradition and emboldened by LeBron's absence, the Bulldogs probably couldn't wait to get on the court for a showdown against our team.

My team's dream of earning a national championship hinged on this game. We were ranked at the top of the *USA Today* national polls, but any stumble would cause us to tumble down the list. We all knew this was the moment of truth. It was also the chance for the rest of the team to strut their stuff. Without LeBron, each player would have the chance to prove his own talents and silence the naysayers that suggested this team was thriving solely off of LeBron's abilities.

"If we were ever unified, we need to be more unified than ever," I said to the team in the locker room before the game. "This is the biggest game of the season, because tomorrow is not promised, and the past is over. This is all we got right now. This is all we got — *right now.* We're a great team with a great player. But this is not a one-man show. This is a great *team.* Don't you ever sell yourself short. I'm just saying words now, but you guys need to go out there and do it on the floor. Play hard, play smart, have fun."

During the game, LeBron sat on the bench, wearing a mustard yellow suit that matched our team's uniform colors. He looked sharp and elegant. The energy at the University of Akron's Rhodes Arena was palpable. As much as fans were there to watch the game, I think they were also there to watch LeBron *watch* the game. The question on everyone's mind hung in the air like smog: can they do it without him?

Right from the start, the Bulldogs showed us that they were determined to win, breaking our press and getting several easy baskets. At times, it seemed like our guys might be overmatched. The team was so used to having LeBron to fall back on. This game became a real test of their strength, stamina, basketball IQ — and even their self-esteem.

Dru III had his warrior persona on full throttle. He moved around the court during the first quarter like someone who was focused on accomplishing a task. He had the same look of unyielding determination in his eyes that he had during his freshman year when he hit those seven three-pointers in a row. Despite being the smallest player physically, he took over the court like it was his and his alone in order to help the team gain a generous lead in the first quarter. I could feel LeBron's satisfaction and pride in his friend.

But the Bulldogs lived up to their name, giving us a real fight. Adding to the handicap of not having LeBron in the game was the fact that Romeo was battling a nasty flu. He wasn't able to play his hardest, even throwing up during some of the time-outs. We had a solid 10-point lead at halftime, but I kept thinking we'd better be ready if anything changed on the court.

During the intermission, Dru gave Romeo one of his "tough love" pep talks. Somehow, Romeo dug even deeper, and his hard work resulted in a 12-point lead at the end of the third quarter. Flu or no flu, Romeo's energy in the fourth quarter kept us safely ahead in the game, 60-50. Despite some last second three-pointers from the Bulldogs, we managed to hold on to win 63-62.

Yes, LeBron's suspension was a lemon of epic proportions. But the sweet lemonade came from the rest of those guys proving to themselves and to the world that their success did not hinge on one player — but instead was the result of being an amazing *team*.

BACK IN BUSINESS

After the pressure of that game eased off, LeBron thought about things and decided to take matters into his own hands. He knew in his heart that he hadn't done anything wrong.

Ignorance of the law was certainly not an excuse, but the penalty didn't match the crime. Where was the grace for a hard-working kid who kept his grades up and always rose above slanderous talk or rumors? Together with his mother, he became intent on figuring out a way to overturn the ruling.

The problem was that in many ways the ruling had a personal element to it. STVM had been having issues with the OHSAA for a while. There was also the fact that Clair Muscaro had publically taken issue with the team's robust schedule during our senior year. More of our games were against teams outside of Ohio than in the state. He was of the belief that our games should be more local. But by that point, we knew that in order to win a national championship we had to travel to play against nationally ranked teams. If we wanted to improve, there was no choice but to leave our comfort zone.

Fed up with the feeling that he was being targeted, LeBron enlisted the aid of a lawyer from Cleveland — the same one who helped them through the Hummer ordeal. A couple of days after the Canton McKinley game, lawyer Frederick Nance filed a motion on LeBron's behalf to stop the association from revoking his eligibility.

At first, Muscaro refused to budge. The main claim against LeBron was that he was trying to capitalize on his celebrity status as an athlete. As I saw it, the real culprits were the media outlets who hunted around for scandalous stories about him like hungry sharks. No one at the OHSAA seemed to understand that if LeBron had really wanted to capitalize, he would have accepted deals with eager sneaker companies and dropped out of school to run his own show. He could have done that at any point. But he was there to play ball with his boys. Nobody seemed to get that, as famous as LeBron was at this point, he still had the heart of a servant when it came to his team.

After the team's fall from grace during its junior year, we weren't about to give up on the dream over a couple of jerseys. (By the way, LeBron had returned the jerseys, even well before our game against McKinley.) Thanks to LeBron's decision to defend himself, things did turn around. On February 5, with swarms of reporters waiting to hear the verdict, a judge in the Summit County court ruled that LeBron's eligibility be immediately restored. According to the judge, the punishment for the infraction was too severe. As of that day, LeBron would be reinstated.

The judge did set two conditions. First, LeBron would still be ineligible for one game, which STVM could choose. And second, the forfeit of a game against Buchtel remained upheld.

Honestly, we were just happy to have our man back. Even STVM ultimately came out in public support for LeBron. Before the judge's ruling, James Burdon, the chairman of the board of trustees at STVM, said: "Our support of LeBron is because of who he is. He's a member of the school community here. In his years as student at STVM, he has excelled academically and socially, as well as athletically. As part of our school community, he deserves our wholehearted support."

Of course we were all delighted with the way things turned out. Even more than that, this whole thing ignited an even deeper fire in LeBron. I knew he'd come back on the court blazing, so to speak.

Our first game after the ruling was against Los Angeles-based Westchester High School in Trenton, New Jersey. At first, it seemed like our players were ready to let it rip, feeling relaxed and happy about having the team intact.

But sometimes, too much emotion can cloud how you play. Westchester took advantage by quickly ramping up a 6-point lead.

It didn't last long, however, because the L-Train was about to start rolling. Romeo got us going, scoring a basket. Then, LeBron swooped in with 18 points that put us in the lead after the first quarter. By halftime he had 31 points. By the end of the game, he had tallied 52! Not only was it his career high, but it also equaled the opposing team's *entire* score for the game, as we won 78-52.

SAVOR THE LEMONADE

We had made lemonade, and LeBron was drinking deeply with his 52-point outburst. In spite of all the lemons we'd had hurled at us during that year:

- the crushing loss in the state championship their junior year
- losing Coach Dambrot
- the media scrutiny
- LeBron's two-game suspension

we had managed to make lemonade. We hurdled — or ran through — every obstacle that was placed before us.

Fame, the team found out, was both a blessing and a curse. By being in the spotlight, they were the target of gossip and criticism. Every victory was picked apart. Every misstep was looked at under a microscope.

At first, the players were targeted because they chose STVM over Buchtel. Then when they'd given their hearts to STVM, they were targeted for becoming too successful. Instead of sulking or feeling like they were being picked on unfairly, they buckled down and focused. They realized their success would be the result of hard work, determination, and the ability to withstand unexpected changes.

Later, we came to realize that the lemons in our path only helped to strengthen our team's resolve. It showed the boys, and anyone who was watching, that they were tough enough to handle anything. Through squeezing the lemons in their lives, the boys grew even closer, worked even harder, and became even more determined to accomplish their dream — which would ultimately be the sweetest lemonade of all.

BEYOND THE COURT

Question: Have you ever felt picked on? How did you handle the situation? Did you pull in a parent for extra help?

Question: What's the biggest "lemon" you've had to deal with in your life? What was the outcome? Would you do anything differently after reading this chapter?

Question: What's the largest "lemon" you can imagine encountering in life? How would it make you feel knowing that you have an almighty God on your side to help you through the situation? Do you lean on God enough in your daily life with your daily problems?

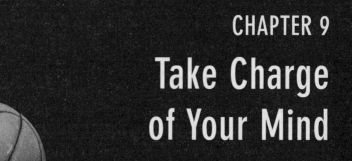

CHAPTER 9

Take Charge of Your Mind

"You can make all the excuses you want, but if you're not mentally tough and you're not prepared to play every night, you're not going to win."[31]

basketball hall of famer Larry Bird

What does your inner monologue tell you?

You'll never amount to anything.

You're better than everybody around you.

You can do it.

Just give up – now.

This pesky, relentless voice creeps into our thoughts and sets up shop like it owns the place. This endlessly chattering voice fills the space of our internal world and, to a large extent, determines not only how we feel but also how we act. It doesn't take a psychologist or neuroscientist to understand the basic idea that if our inner monologue is laced with negative thoughts, then negativity will seep into how we talk and behave. This is why the *tone* of our thoughts is so crucial.

Think about it: if you play a song all day long that contains nothing but the sound of harsh static or shrill sirens, by the end of the day, you'll feel terrible. Your brain will yearn for some peace and quiet. While this might be an extreme example, it should give you some indication of what happens when you allow your mind to be filled with all kinds of negative self-talk.

Thankfully, the opposite is also true. If we load our minds with positive thoughts, that positivity will overflow into our disposition and actions. To counter the screeching sounds, let's say you listen to the sounds of waterfalls or ocean waves all day long. Likely, at the end of the day, your mind will be calm and peaceful.

Both examples reflect the power of our inner voice. Positive thoughts lead to calmness and joy. Negative thoughts jar our minds, ending in tension and depression.

While negativity and positivity are opposites, they do have something in common. Both have the power to dictate the flow of a person's life. The Bible tells it straight in Philippians 4:8 – 9: "Finally, brothers and sisters, whatever is true, whatever is noble, whatever is right, whatever is pure, whatever is lovely, whatever is admirable — if anything is excellent or praiseworthy — think about such things. Whatever you have learned or received or heard from me, or seen from me — put it into practice. And the God of peace will be with you."

It sounds simple enough, right? *Just don't have bad thoughts.* But by trying not to think any bad thoughts, it almost causes you to think a bad thought. It's a paradox.

Have you ever tried to pray for five minutes straight? What happened? For the first minute, you might have stayed on track, thanking God for how He provides for and loves you.

But pretty soon you're unintentionally thinking about that math test or what you should've said to your best friend. If trying to control our minds for five minutes of focused mediation on God seems impossible, how can we take the reins of our volatile inner monologue?

I won't lie. It's not easy. But let's look at a few steps that can be taken to dig deep and really take charge of our minds.

Left to its own devices, the mind is like an unruly, untamed beast. It leaps abruptly from one idea to the next. It's more advanced than a supercomputer. But it sometimes has difficulty recalling even a simple history fact. This beast can be aggressive, clumsy, unclear, and downright troublesome.

But here's some good news. Have you ever seen a big dog that dutifully walks beside its owner? Despite its size and stature, a big dog can be trained to bend to its master's commands. It knows that it is the master who leads the way and calls the shots. This beast does not pounce, does not howl, and does not pull the master this way or that. Instead, the master leads it down a path that makes sense. Such are the qualities of a mind that's under control.

Ideally, we are the masters of our minds — not vice versa. In a perfect world, we are able to dictate where our thoughts go and how much power they have over us. But like a dog who walks its master, it often feels like our thoughts take us places we don't want to go. So what are some ways we can become masters of our mind?

CONTROL WHAT YOU CAN CONTROL

Have you ever heard the "Serenity Prayer"? Written by Reinhold Niebuhr in the twentieth century, it begins by saying:

God grant me the serenity to accept the things I cannot change; the courage to change the things I can; and the wisdom to know the difference.[32]

These words perfectly explain the concept that I like to call, "controlling what you can control." If you aim to master your mind, it's a concept you should take seriously.

But *how* do we do this? It begins with the practice of turning inward and applying our focus to the things that we *can* control, which are our thoughts, perceptions, attitudes, words, and actions.

Notice I didn't include *feelings* on this list. To a certain degree, we really cannot control our feelings. Sometimes, we just wake up feeling a little mournful or depressed without even knowing why.

While we may not necessarily be able to control our feelings, what we *can* do is observe them. We can watch them as they crop up. Do our feelings properly reflect the situation? Are we reacting properly, or is there too much emotion behind our feelings? We must focus on this crucial truth the whole time: feelings are not facts.

So let's get back to those things we can control — our thoughts, perceptions, attitudes, words, and actions. How do we keep our focus on these? Proverbs 4:25 – 26 says it best: "Let your eyes look straight ahead; fix your gaze directly before you. Give careful thought to the paths for your feet and be steadfast in all your ways."

This means we have an individual duty to keep our eyes fixed on our purpose, to identify the pathways to those objectives, and to steadily move in the right direction. When we live in line with our purpose, we are like a flower that blossoms fully each day. When we don't, we live in a permanent state of being wilted. By focusing our minds on our dreams, we make less room for the negative voices. By filling our consciousness with thoughts and ideas about how to make our dreams come true, we stamp out the fires of doubt and fear. When we utilize our energy for making progress in our lives, we leave less energy in our reservoir for negativity.

I know it all sounds great on paper. But life is not lived as words in a book. Our minds inevitably take over multiple times a day, or even every hour. I had to work insanely hard to take charge of my mind, especially in the context of coaching.

So many personalities and variables factor into each workout, each practice, each team, and each game. I find myself having to constantly control my mind so I don't add to the situation with my own burst of emotion. Sometimes, there's a player who loves to talk back, or a ref who seems keen on making questionable calls, or a know-it-all parent who thinks he can run my team more effectively, or an opposing team that comes onto the court with a little too much aggression.

What do all these things have in common? They are all external circumstances, which means they are outside of my control.

Instead of getting bent out of shape over variables that exist beyond me, I tell myself to channel my energy toward something that matters to me, such as:

- my spiritual commitment to live a Christian life
- my professional goal of teaching young men how to collaborate as a team
- my intention to be a loving husband and father

An ineffective me, one consumed by outside forces, would stomp around in anger, huffing and puffing about the injustices I feel like I'm facing. A more effective me, however, sees that there isn't enough anger in the world to change these things. Instead of ranting, I exert every bit of my mental power toward keeping my goals and values clear. In this way, I diffuse seemingly bad situations with the power of my own conviction.

Sometimes it's harder than others. Given the notoriety of the team, LeBron's ascension to superstardom, and the sheer momentum of our success, I was front and center for the media to devour. Devour they did, often leaving me enraged by their scrutiny, thinking, *I'm just a high school coach.*

But in order to lead my team properly, I'd shake it off and remind myself that I was coaching a group of boys who were in the national spotlight. As fulfilling as it could be, it also came with the price of my anonymity. I had to shelve any hurt feelings and realize that part of being the coach of a high-profile team meant taking the brunt of the media's attacks.

Players are the ones who win games, but it's coaches who lose them. Even though I have always sort of known this, I make a point to remind myself of this truth every morning. Every loss brings a new invitation to be second-guessed. No matter how I slice it, coaching has given me a crash course on the art of letting things go and controlling where my mind goes.

SET YOUR OWN COURSE

You know what else you can control? Your trajectory. Your path. Your route toward your destiny. It's not enough to let things go and stand proud of who you are. Those are both great, but ultimately, you still have to go out there and execute.

To really take charge of your mind, you have a responsibility to put yourself in the driver's seat, leading the expedition of your life in the direction that God is calling *you.*

Sometimes, even our closest relationships can dampen that

path. It's not that our friends or loved ones don't want us to succeed. They just happen to see the world — and how you might fit into it — differently. I can't tell you how many kids I come across who are gung-ho about being college basketball players. Some practically dribble a basketball in their sleep. Yet, when push comes to shove and they have to let go of a way of life or a group of friends for the sake of their dream, they cave. Social sacrifice can often be part of staying dedicated to your dream.

I'll never forget this one friend that Dru III had as a child. His name was Kenneth. Starting around second grade, those two were inseparable. They were always at one another's houses playing, horsing around, or just watching TV. My son loved being with his friend — that is, until Dru III discovered basketball. Then he loved basketball more. Very quickly, all of his time and energy got poured into the sport. Naturally, the closer Dru got to basketball, the farther away he drifted from Kenneth. There wasn't a fight or an argument over the change. Each understood, in a rather mature way, that their paths were taking different directions.

Kenneth ended up going into the military, which has its own set of rigors and demands. Though the boys didn't hold onto the closeness of their youth, they stayed in touch. Even today, they hold a respect for one another, knowing that each did what he had to do in order to walk his true path.

Mind the Books

A problem I see all the time is that students put athletics above academics. The truth is that almost always it's in your best interest to put academics first. If you're going to take charge of your mind, you must get it firmly focused on the classroom. Not only are there academic eligibility requirements to worry about, but what you learn now will serve you for the rest of your life as well.

I don't mean to sound like a broken record, but there's only one LeBron. I should know. After coaching him, I've become somewhat of a magnet to young men (and their parents) who believe they're the next one. They're not. While I've been fortunate to coach some great players since LeBron left St. Vincent-St. Mary, suffice it to say that none have come close to duplicating his ability.

Almost to a man, they all would have been better off putting more effort into academics. That's not a knock against anyone's game. Rather, it's an accurate assessment of the realities in the world.

Unless your basketball skill set and athletic ability are in the top one percent, you will probably have ten or twenty times more earning potential by staying academically focused.

The NBA creates hundreds of millionaires every year. But in 2013, 9,600,000 millionaires lived in the United States.[33] That means millions of people have been able to make a very good living outside of sports.

So as odd as this might sound coming from a basketball coach, when you put all your eggs in the sports basket, you are greatly limiting your potential.

Once Dru III found basketball, he found other friends who shared his passion and dedication to the sport. The Fab Five turned out to be more than friends — they became his family. For Dru and Kenneth, their distance happened early on, but it's not always so easy.

When I say taking charge of your mind means learning to let go, I'm not just talking about negative thoughts or incidents. Sometimes it's also about certain people. You have to step away from any individuals who consistently don't support you or try to distract you from your goals. If you have a friend who challenges your God-honoring objectives and makes you feel bad about your choices (especially if they're encouraging you toward negative behaviors), that's one you should let go of. That might sound harsh. But look at it as pruning your own garden so that your soul has room to really grow.

As a coach, I often remind my players that this is their journey — and theirs alone.

"You're not here because of me," I say. "You're not here because of your parents or your friends. You're here because you want to be here. So show me. But more important, you've got to show that to *yourself.*"

Each student is on a distinct journey, one riddled with factors and circumstances that give it direction. It's already hard enough to know what God's will is for our lives. Oftentimes, getting some distance from a relationship that's blurring the way can help.

Relationships will come and go. After all, we're social creatures. As we go through life, we'll be part of different groups, teams, cliques, circles, and networks of people. Whole new casts of characters come into our lives at the start of a new school year or during the transition into college. Some friends will stick with us and encourage us throughout our lives. But people will come and go for different reasons.

This concept is hard for young people to grasp because they often value friendships over their own dreams. They allow themselves to stay stuck. Instead of soaring to their potential, the comfort of what they know swallows them up.

Please don't get me wrong. I'm not saying relationships are not meaningful. But remember that everything changes. Relationships are no different. They are subject to the ebb and flow of life, just like anything else.

If you are unable to leave behind friends who drag you down, you may never reach your full potential. In any field, once you decide you want to pursue it, you have to make sacrifices. Some students just can't pull themselves away from their old neighborhood. They get sucked into a vortex where the cool thing to do is to *do nothing*. Whatever sliver of promise they had gets hijacked by the distractions of static space.

As you move along your road to success, don't be surprised if some of your old "friends" play the oh-you're-too-good-for-us-now card. When that happens, you have to be able to separate yourself and say, "I don't believe I'm too good for you. I'm just going in a different direction."

You can never really leave *true* friends behind, because if they're real friends, they will never try to impede your journey. They will instead evolve right along your side to encourage and support you. Real friends often become your number one fans.

That said, when it comes to letting things go, it works the other way, too. Sometimes people come into our lives who at first we want nothing to do with. Maybe their personalities grate against ours or they appear to have little in common with us. It's only after a little time has passed that we realize these individuals were meant to come into our lives for a very significant reason.

Take Romeo Travis, for example. When he joined the team as a transfer student during his sophomore year, he was viewed as an outsider. He was a difficult young man — part rebel, part loner, and all grit. He referred to himself as "angry man." I can't really blame him. He had a tough upbringing and was still working through a lot of stuff.

As hard as it was for the other players to see how Romeo fit into their team, it was also rough for Romeo. This group of guys was so close they were practically brothers. They had their own lingo, their inside jokes, and their way of interacting with one another. They were a tiny universe unto themselves.

Romeo's attitude presented the Fab Four with a dilemma. On the one hand, they couldn't stand this newcomer, who was unsettling the balance of their perfect foursome. But as much as they didn't appreciate his swagger or intimidation tactics, they very much liked his game.

Romeo showed his rare abilities as a ballplayer during his first year on the team in one of our most important games. We were playing against Buchtel, the school the Fab Four had been expected to attend before Dru III felt led to play for Coach Dambrot at STVM. They made a lot of enemies by choosing to play at STVM instead. This was their first game played against Buchtel so, needless to say, emotions ran high in the James Rhodes arena that night.

Maybe it was the pressure or the emotion of this particular game, but the boys just didn't have their groove. At halftime, Buchtel led 37-36. It was only a 1-point deficit, but all of us were starting to feel the weight of a loss already descending on our shoulders.

That's when LeBron and Romeo kicked into high gear. They hit back-to-back baskets to help us regain the lead. We ended up winning 58-50 — and a lot of it had to do with Romeo's big push at the end.

At six-feet-six-inches, Romeo was an excellent offensive player. With powerful low-post moves and great leaping ability, he was a force inside. Add to that the fact that LeBron was already proving himself to be an all-time great at throwing lob passes, and they quickly became a formidable duo. Romeo also used his leaping ability to control the game as a shot blocker, which led to fast breaks and plenty of memorable dunks for LeBron. So despite their off-court differences, on the court, Romeo was exactly what the team needed. And everybody knew it.

In this case, the team had no choice but to collectively take charge of their minds and accept Romeo for what he was — a huge asset and a teammate they must support. If their number one priority was *the team*, they would have to shelve the off-court issues for the sake of the group's success. They would have to dig into their own sense of empathy and try to understand Romeo's point of view as someone who never felt part of anything until he was a part of this team.

For Romeo's part, he, too, would have to let go of the belief that he was destined to forever be an outsider. He'd have to soften up a bit, not be so intensely brash, and open up himself to his teammates. Ultimately, Romeo would have to be a team player if he wanted to be a player on the team.

In the end, that's what happened. Romeo became the "Plus One" to the Fab Four. He shared enough glory and fond memories with his teammates that they are still close today. In fact, during the summer of 2014 when everybody was speculating where LeBron would end up after his second free agency, he made headlines by showing up at his skills academy in Las Vegas. And who did he take the court with? Dru III and Romeo.

They're all older and more mature today, but they deserve tremendous credit for refusing to get stuck in a negative situation during their high school years. They went from literally pummeling one another, on and off the court, to working together to teach young boys about the game of basketball — all because they put their pettiness aside and took charge of their minds.

THE PARENT TRAP

Unfortunately, friends are not the only ones who may be obstacles. Sometimes, it's the adults — parents even — who, despite having the best intentions, find a way to get in the way. And I'm no exception.

Managing the roles of father and coach to Dru III created a lot of tension for me … and for him. Many times, I pushed my son so hard that he ended up in tears. When I saw him break down, I asked myself if I was going too far, demanding too much. Ultimately, I reconciled my toughness on him with the fact that:

1. He loved this game more than anything in his life.
2. We both had to prove our skills to ourselves and to everyone watching, irrespective of our father-son ties.

That meant he had to be good enough to earn his court time so people wouldn't think he was playing because I was coaching. I made plenty of missteps during that period, but I believe we can both say the stumbles were worth the incredible journey we experienced through basketball.

Most parents want what's best for their kids. Sometimes, in their zeal to get their children ahead, they press them too hard or create expectations that are not in line with the child's own dream. Other times, the expectations are simply unattainable.

On too many occasions, I have met young people being forced to follow other people's dreams instead of pursuing what truly inspires them. Maybe basketball was the kid's dream when he was nine or ten years old, but now he's fifteen and has other interests. I have coached many players whose hearts weren't in basketball, yet they found themselves forced to play the game because their parents loved it. I encourage those players to make the most of their time playing basketball but to also pursue their true passions. In addition, I counsel the parents to accept their child's dream, even if it doesn't match their own.

But parents don't deserve all the blame. The parent-child relationship is just that … a relationship. There has to be open and honest communication. You can't stew inside, growing angrier and angrier at your parent for forcing you to do something if you don't express what truly excites you. Tell your parents what activities you gravitate toward more naturally. Ask them to help you nurture the skills you need to get ahead and to find your own place in society.

And here's the key: don't wait until you explode in a fit of rage. The Bible says, "Honor your father and mother" (Ephesians 6:2). Try to talk calmly to your parents if your goals for life differ from theirs. Be open to their input. They may see gifts and abilities that you didn't know you had. Show them respect.

At the same time, it's a two-way street. The Bible also says, "And you, fathers, do not provoke your children to wrath" (Ephesians 6:4, NKJV). Your parents should be asking themselves: "Am I really nurturing *this* child's nature?" Making it through to adulthood is a team effort. When you work together with your parents as a team, you'll end up with the best results.

If I'm being honest, I had to ask myself some tough questions when neither Dru III nor Cameron was highly recruited out of high school. For a moment, I thought maybe I could have done things differently. But at the same time, I knew basketball was their dream — not my dream for them. Since they were willing to work, I helped them. But they had to control their minds and block out the naysayers to make it in the sport. Over and over again, I reminded them: "It's *your* dream."

I'm not trying to turn any child against his family. My desire is for students and parents to talk about their goals — on the court or off — and develop a plan to make those goals a reality. You've got to employ a razor-sharp focus, which goes back to taking charge of your own mind. If you do that, in the end, you and your parents will be happy.

THE DOCTRINE OF RELATIVE FILTH

Another crucial lesson to learn on the road to taking charge of your mind is to avoid comparing yourself to others. Each person has his own unique thoughts, feelings, reactions, upbringing, geography, physicality, circumstances, and more. Because everybody is fundamentally different, comparing ourselves to one another is completely futile. Comparison often breeds contempt. We may become jealous of somebody else's abilities or position in life. Or we can become bigheaded and overestimate our own status. Either way, comparison is a monumental waste of our time and energy.

My youngest son, Cameron, was overlooked by many college recruiters because of his height. He struggled with accepting the fact that players he had outperformed were receiving scholarships to top colleges. He used to get upset, saying, "But I gave that guy the business when we were matched up. How could he get an offer over me?" or "I locked that guy down when we played. Why are they more interested in him?"

While it was easy to understand Cameron's frustration, ultimately, he had to understand that he wasn't gaining anything by worrying about someone else's situation. Maybe it wasn't fair. But any energy put into stewing over those questions was ultimately wasted energy.

Cameron realized that, changed his attitude, and began pouring all of his energy and mental focus into his own play. It was only then that he earned a scholarship to play basketball at Northwood University, a Division II school in Michigan. As of 2014, he's an assistant coach there.

Comparison works the other way too. Years ago, I attended a program called "Character Counts" (see www.charactercounts .com). This educational seminar centered around six pillars:

1. trustworthiness
2. respect
3. responsibility
4. fairness
5. caring
6. citizenship

During this program, I first learned about the doctrine of relative filth. Essentially, this is a type of rationalization used by people to minimize their moral deficiencies by comparing themselves to others with even lower standards.

We've all done it. Have you ever found yourself thinking, *I'm just going to try one beer. It's not like I'm like Mitchell. He gets drunk every weekend.* Or maybe you've been sent to detention for being late to class and thought, *I can't believe I'm going to detention. Leslie ditches all the time, and she never gets in trouble.*

Just because your friends copy answers from each other's homework, doesn't make it right for you to cheat on a test. But many people attempt to rationalize their misdeeds by pointing to their peers and claiming, "Well, it's not as bad as what they're doing."

I encounter this all the time with my players. If I reprimand one for not getting back on defense, I rarely hear, "Got it, Coach." Instead, he'll reply with, "Well, John didn't get back either. How come you're not saying anything to him?"

"Because John's shortcomings don't have anything to do with yours," I sometimes explain. "Maybe I've already had the same conversation with John. Or maybe I told John to crash the offensive boards, making it harder for him to get back on defense. There could be any number of reasons. But none of them affect the message I'm giving to *you*."

Sadly, our culture is all about pointing fingers. Nobody seems willing to take responsibility for his or her actions. It's always somebody else's fault, or they want special treatment. All you have to do is look at politics or entertainment icons to see how it plays out every day. But like I always tell my guys, "Whenever you point a finger, there are three of them pointing right back at you."

The bottom line is that we must avoid carrying around other people's drama or trying to use missteps for our own benefit. We have an obligation to not allow other people's subpar behavior to be justification for our own negative actions.

To take control of our minds, we must be able to shut out the negative voices around us and instead focus on our own gifts. Only then will we be more likely to gain the confidence and self-esteem we need in order to navigate the rough stretches of life.

As I continue to mature as a man and follower of Christ, I've come to realize one of the keys to leading a successful life is changing my perceptions of situations. Every experience can lead to personal growth. By releasing my need to control things and embracing a situation as a learning opportunity, I can begin to gain self-control. And self-control leads to a multitude of other benefits.

The apostle Peter wrote a step-by-step account in the Bible on how to grow into a more balanced, joyful person[34] — the kind of person who can let things go, set their own course, shut out the negative voices, accept outsiders, and take responsibility for their actions.

Peter says it all starts with faith. To faith, you must add goodness. Goodness needs a supply of knowledge, and knowledge must have self-control. By having self-control, you develop perseverance to never give up. That singular determination leads to godliness, which ends up in mutual affection for your friends, family members, and teammates. Ultimately, by following that path, you end up at love.

Not a love, like "I love barbecued ribs" or "I love the Miami Heat," but a deep, sustaining, abiding love that never changes. It's a kind of love that affects how you see yourself and the world around you — a love that helps you take charge of your own mind.

BEYOND THE COURT

Question: Are there any negative thoughts you need to take control of? How can focusing on good or positive things change the atmosphere of your mind?

Question: Do you have any friends who are holding you back from moving forward in achieving your dreams? What course of action can you take?

Question: Why is comparison so dangerous? Think about ways to judge yourself by your own actions, not by the actions of the people around you.

CHAPTER 10

Dare to Dream

"God is a God of excellence, so that's just what we have to give back to him — excellence."[35]

Bishop Joey Johnson

Whatever success I've achieved, I've had to work very hard for. When I look back on my childhood in East Liverpool, I can't help but feel blessed. I've come a long, long way from the ramshackle house with a leaky roof on a treacherous dirt road. The house I live in sits in a nice suburb. I can't even compare the black sedan I drive today to the car my family had back then, because we didn't have a car!

This success was realized through the implementation of all the principles I've previously unpacked — decisions, mentorship, self-empowerment, discipline, servitude, communication, perspective, and determination. But success also happened because of something that sits somewhere between our imagination and our potential — it's *our dreams*.

I give tremendous credit to my family for, perhaps even unknowingly, helping me to catapult my dreams into reality. My parents sacrificed their own time and interests, just so I could have a decent life. They also saw the value of putting me on a plane every summer to visit with my sister, JoAnne, in New York. Thanks to my parents' permission and my sister's willingness to expose me to "the bigger world," I learned what it means to yearn for more in life.

First of all, I saw my sister's determination in action. She left home at an early age, took charge of her own mind, and created an entirely new life for herself. And second, just being in New York, a place that many would call the center of the universe, fueled me with inspiration and a sense of possibility.

As far as dreaming goes, those early years laid some important groundwork for me. They gave me the ability to see different possibilities in life, ones that were far removed from anything I knew. Leaving East Liverpool each summer forced me out of my comfort zone and invited me to think outside the box. The more expansive my perspective became, the more I was able to zero in on my true nature, map out the role I wanted to play in the world, and tap into my dreams.

If I really strip it down, I have had two fundamental dreams — both of which felt entirely out of reach at different points in my life. One was the dream of being a father and a husband. The other was the dream of being a coach.

While I was a college student spending my time chasing girls and getting high, the very last thing I ever imagined I would achieve was being a father and a husband. It seemed as far away from me as the moon. My daily behavior at that time only served to push it farther away. I wasn't living as my true self. I was living as a fool. But thanks to a significant emotional event and the grace of God, I was able to turn from my destructive ways and receive forgiveness from Carolyn, who's been my loving wife and greatest support all these years.

It was only by giving her the respect and place that she deserved in my life that I was able to create what I always knew would be my greatest accomplishment: my family.

And once I became a father and a husband, the last thing I was going to do was let down my wife and children. There was no room for selfishness. Just as my parents sacrificed for me, I'd sacrifice for my family. The Bible says, "Anyone who does not provide for their relatives, and especially for their own household, has denied the faith and is worse than an unbeliever" (1 Timothy 5:8). Those are strong words. The responsibility of fatherhood is a high calling.

I determined to do everything in my power to give my family a great life, even if that meant staying in an unfulfilling job for years. I continue to be grateful for the time I spent at ConAgra, because despite the feeling of dissatisfaction in my day-to-day duties, it gave us financial security during our first twenty-five years of marriage.

Needless to say, my life journey has felt like a miracle of epic proportions. Besides seeing God's guiding hand at key points in my life, the one ingredient that truly made it possible was the fact that I allowed myself to dream.

When you think about dreams, you may first picture the stuff that pops into your head when you're asleep. But the more powerful dreams are the dreams in our lives that we *wake up* to. These dreams come to us as revelations of our true selves. Your dreams may start as tiny seeds. Made up of part hope, part desire, and part wanting to connect with your truest self, you must plant this dream in your heart and never give up in nurturing it to sprout and grow in your life.

THE FAITH WALK

Typically, dreams aren't realized overnight, nor do they happen on their own. So what does it take to make your dreams come true?

In my experience, it begins with really listening to the whispers of your heart. Whispers are quiet. You often can't hear them amidst the noise that surrounds our lives. You must unplug from the world around you. Put down your smartphone, pause the music in your headphones, get off the computer, step out of the gym, and walk away from the video games. Just stop and simply listen to the Creator. Call it meditation, call it prayer, call it whatever you want — but the answers we seek reveal themselves during this very special and crucial time.

When I speak of your heart, I am referring to your unconscious mind. This is a place of great mystery, but also of great truth. In some ways, it's much more advanced than the conscious mind — because it knows more than we consciously understand. We have to tap into this great mystery and find a way to articulate the way the heart is directing. As for me, that "heart direction" came when I heard God's voice — one that emanated from stillness and serenity that could only really come from a deep place within my soul.

Heart Versus Gut

If you've seen even a single Disney movie, you've probably heard somebody say, "Follow your heart."

That may work for Disney princes and princesses, but it may not be too effective in the real world. In the Scriptures, the Lord tells the prophet Jeremiah (17:9), "The heart is deceitful above all things and beyond cure. Who can understand it?" That's a pretty strong warning *not* to follow your heart. You can't really trust or control your *feelings*, which is what most people use when they go with their heart. The wisest man who ever lived, King Solomon, put it this way, "He who trusts in his own heart is a fool, but whoever walks wisely will be delivered" (Proverbs 28:26, NKJV).

So instead of trusting in your heart, it's better advice to "use your head, and go with your gut."

In the ancient world, including during biblical times, the gut was the center of love and compassion — not the heart. The Greeks especially believed our emotions resided in our gut. Maybe that's why we get "butterflies in our stomach" when we're nervous or why some great athletes throw up before games. NBA all-time great Bill Russell got so nervous before games that he regularly lost his lunch before stepping onto the hardwood. He helped the Boston Celtics win eleven NBA championships, so his teammates looked at his vomiting as a sign of good luck.[36]

The next time you're faced with a tough decision or don't know the next step in your life, stop to think and then trust your gut. Just make sure your direction isn't being swayed by having indigestion.

So when I did decide to leave my consistent job at ConAgra, my mind was not flooded with doubt. Instead, a flurry of ideas and possibilities came to me as to how to craft my new plan. With that certainty and clarity, I left my job of twenty-five years and began a walk of faith.

I knew if I didn't show the courage to be my most authentic

self, things would only get worse. Taking a monumental risk in walking away from the comfort of stability demanded my utmost trust in God and a ton of hard work.

God is the giver and keeper of our dreams. It is through our interaction with him that we are able to realize our dreams. In this dynamic relationship with God, sometimes you must "take the lead" with your effort and attitude. Then God guides you through His divine providence. Some people call it coincidence, but it's through God's hand that opportunities and people come into our lives at the perfect time.

Unexplainable things fall into place in all of our lives. When those unexplainable things seem to open doors or move obstacles, it's not that the universe is simply smiling on you. The truth is that the Creator is active in your life, and you need to acknowledge God's hand in your walk. Know that it is him leading those moments of the dance.

As I left the security of my former job and stepped into coaching, God's providence was clear. The more I acknowledged His work, the more I began to see His movements in those unexplainable moments.

In December 2003, I went to Dru III's first college game at the University of Akron. The Zips were playing the Cincinnati Bearcats. The Cincinnati roster included four players from Texas and just one from Ohio.

Why is that? I thought. I didn't think any state had better players than Ohio.

I found someone who wrote for a recruiting service and asked, "Why is Ohio so underrepresented on the Cincinnati bench? The school is in our own backyard. Certainly, they know how good our players are."

He explained that even though Cincinnati was close geographically, the coaches might not be aware of all the local talent. An NCAA rule at the time only allowed Division I coaches to evaluate players during the month of April in events sanctioned by each state's governing body for high school athletics.

"The Texas Athletic Association sanctions April tournaments," he said. "The Ohio High School Athletic Association (OHSAA) doesn't."

In my opinion, that explained why Ohio was being under-recruited and how Texas players had more opportunities to earn spots on Division I college rosters.

"So what would it take to get the OHSAA to approve an event and give our kids a better chance?" I asked.

"A politician," he replied, laughing.

Not knowing much about the political arena, but wanting to give Ohio basketball players a better chance to play Division I basketball, I sought help to make this kind of tournament happen. Two years later, the city of Akron and some business leaders were on board, but I still couldn't get a meeting with the commissioner of the OHSAA.

I may have gotten the ball rolling, but that's when God began to lead in the dance. Out of nowhere, Larry Long contacted me about some insurance. Larry was from East Liverpool (talk about "coincidence"). As a kid, I had watched Larry's dad play football, and later Larry had watched me. He asked me how coaching was going. I shared that I wanted to create a travel team basketball event to showcase Ohio high school players but that I needed the OHSAA to sanction the event, so Division I coaches could attend.

"Dru," Larry said with excitement in his voice, "the Speaker Pro Tempore of the Ohio House of Representatives, Chuck Blasdel, lives in East Liverpool."

He went on to explain that Chuck grew up in Akron

and his dad was a long-time girls' basketball coach at Akron Central-Hower High School. Larry didn't stop there. Chuck was planning to run for a U.S. House of Representative seat and was having a cookout to announce his candidacy. Larry invited me to attend and to meet Chuck that weekend.

I went to the cookout, and things happened faster than I ever imagined they could. When I explained how I wanted to showcase Ohio basketball players, Chuck immediately asked his aide to set up a meeting with the commissioner of the OHSAA.

By Monday, I had all the details of the meeting in Columbus. God was not finished. The meeting took place in October of 2005 in the offices of Representative Blasdel. I explained to Commissioner Daniel Ross how important the travel team tournaments were in the recruiting process. The commissioner listened intently and then posed a question, "Dru, do you have the support of the Ohio High School Basketball Coaches Association?"

"I don't," I admitted.

"Well, without their support, there's no way I could sanction the event," he said.

The meeting adjourned. Now, I needed to get the coaches association on board before the tournament could go any further. We left the conference room, and Chuck asked us into his office. As Chuck heard the details, he asked if there was any way I could get the coaches association's support.

A name immediately popped into my mind: Norm Persin.

I'd met Norm during the summer of 2004 when Nike sent me to work the Michael Jordan Basketball Camp. I went to learn how to plan and execute a world-class basketball camp, as I was to about to start a camp for LeBron. But as I sat in Chuck's office, I clearly understood that the Lord had been orchestrating my steps all along. He had sent me to Jordan's camp specifically to meet Norm. He was a veteran Ohio high school basketball coach and a former president of the coaches association, and we hit it off immediately. If there was anyone who could get the coaches association to support my idea, it would be him.

Norm agreed with what I was trying to do.

"I'm no longer president of the coaches association," he said, "but the leadership tends to listen to me."

Norm explained that the next meeting was in November. He would share my idea and let me know their decision. A few weeks later, Norm called with the answer. "Yes!" he said.

Once the coaches were on board, Commissioner Ross gave his support, and we received a formal letter sanctioning our event on January 2, 2006. At the time, it was the first sanctioned event in the Midwest.

In 2014, the King James Shooting Stars Classic finished its ninth year. We have grown from an amazing 318 teams the first year (I say *amazing* because we got that number in three months) to an event that consistently has 500-plus teams. The tournament generates upward of $2 million for the local economy.

As I said before, God honors effort. Ten years ago, I never could have imagined I would be doing what I'm doing. Now we're up to five events, and we're developing partnerships. I wake up each morning excited about the day, eager to solve problems and face obstacles. I feel empowered, capable, and passionate.

The basketball tournaments are a blessing straight from God. Not only do they allow thousands of players from Ohio to showcase their talents in front of top college coaches, but they also help provide for my family. Let me be clear: you can't be a high school coach if you're in it for the money. When people hear what I make at STVM, they're shocked. Let's just say you couldn't live off that salary if you were a single guy with no one depending on you. But if you follow your dreams for the right reasons, God's blessings will come. The money might not be there right away, but God never fails to provide for those who follow His will.

Today, I am clear about my motivations. The basketball tournaments allow me to continue to coach. As I live out my dreams, I'm also being an example to young men. On the one hand, I am there to coach them and develop their talents on the court. But they also see what I've been able to create from a business point of view, so they recognize that great things can be created if you work hard.

A DREAM DEFERRED

"What happens to a dream deferred? Does it dry up like a raisin in the sun?"[37] This quote from the poem "Harlem" by Langston Hughes does a good job describing an experience I had while writing this book. One of my former players had a very close relative murdered. I went to the wake to support him and his family.

The church was located on a narrow street. The outpouring from the community was massive. Cars were parked three and four blocks away in every direction. I saw a lot of young people I had not seen in a long time — former athletes who had dreamed of playing professionally, single mothers who had dreamed of college, and young men who had turned to selling drugs because they lacked marketable skills.

As I spoke to many of them, it saddened me to discover that they had not fulfilled their dreams. They seemed to have aged quickly and lost hope. All of the dreams and excitement that had sparked them as children were gone.

But dreams, no matter how large or small can be rekindled with faith and effort. The world is filled with endless possibilities. What may look impossible can still be achievable if you begin to recognize positive opportunities in your life. Daily decisions can create the possibility for you to grow and eventually grasp hold of your goals.

Dreams have to be nurtured. Sometimes, this process takes a long time. Bumps in the road may present themselves. But you cannot allow the bumps to cause you to give up.

That is what I saw at the wake — people who had given up. It made me so sad. Too many people stop pursuing their dreams when life throws them a curve. We have to learn to persist through the obstacles. Like I said before, we have to believe that everything depends upon God, and work as if everything depends on us.

By the way, my wife, Carolyn, has been a great example to me as someone who never gave up on her dream. Growing up, she had always dreamed of being a designer. She never pursued that passion because her family felt it was too risky a career choice. She went to earn a bachelor's degree in political science from the University of Pittsburgh. Over the years, she tried her hands at other professions but never found something that satisfied her.

Finally, after realizing God had blessed her with a gift, she went back to college to earn a second degree in interior design. Even though she is decades older than most of her fellow students, she's thrown herself into her schoolwork and is positioned to graduate with honors. Her story is a true testament to the fact that we'll always be happiest when we go after the dream God has given us ... even if it takes years to accomplish.

ALONE AT THE TOP

Speaking of years invested into a dream, during the spring of 2003, we had earned the right to play for the national championship. As you may know, a legitimate national high school basketball championship doesn't exist. There's no high school equivalent to NCAA basketball's March Madness. But through year-end tournaments and national rankings, every year a high school team is crowned as the best in the nation.

When we stepped on the floor on March 22, 2003, to face Kettering Ohio's Archbishop Alter, we stood at the top of the *USA Today* national polls. We'd played a national schedule, beating perennial powers Oak Hill Academy from Virginia and Mater Dei from California. A victory in the Division II Ohio state championships would cement our place on top.

As seniors, Dru III, LeBron, and all the guys had endured who knows how many drills, workouts, practices, wins, losses, fights, arguments, attitude adjustments, and a million other travails. We had overcome legal battles, media scrutiny, and the kind of fame that would make most young men go off the deep end. But the goal had not yet been attained. The dream was not yet realized. We still had to defeat a talented and well-coached team from Dayton, Ohio.

"You have the chance to go down as the greatest high school team in basketball history, which is a legacy that's going to be around long after you guys are gone," I said to them as we huddled in the locker room before the game. "We're taking it full circle fellas."

Every member of the team had his head bowed. A feeling of solemnity hung thick in the air. Our hearts pumped with adrenaline, nostalgia, and the desire to finish what we had started so many years ago.

"This all started in a little Salvation Army gym with a lino-leum floor on Maple Street," I continued. "All the travel we have done, from the time you guys were eleven years old — all the way across the country. All the work you put out through high school will culminate when that bus pulls up tomor-row — where at? On Maple Street. The only question right now is: when you get off that bus tomorrow, will you walk off victorious?"

As wound up as I was for the game, I felt a surge of pride watching my players make their entrance onto the court. All of them linked their arms in a cluster of closeness. Once they'd gone through pregame drills and it was time for player introductions, the players had another ritual. They formed two lines, and one-by-one, each player ran through the center of the lines, giving low-fives to his fellow teammates. At the end, he leapt into the air to bump chests with the guy who had gone before him. Not only was it a symbolic acknowledge-ment of their individual significance, but it also showed their unity as a team. It was their way of establishing and honoring their brotherhood.

No matter how motivated and determined the boys were, Kettering wasn't messing around either. They had come into the game with a well-planned strategy to neutralize our speed and athleticism. In a word, they *stalled*.

Because high school basketball doesn't have a shot clock, every time Kettering would get the ball, they would patiently pass the ball around the perimeter, passing and cutting until someone would be out of position and frustrated. The NBA has a twenty-four second shot clock, which means a team has to shoot in that allotted time or the ball is given to their oppo-nent. The NCAA started using a shot clock in 1985, giving teams forty-five seconds to shoot. That was dropped down to thirty-five seconds in 1993.[38] But high school basketball has never adopted the shot clock, so teams can stall for as long as they want. And that's exactly what Kettering did.

The Knights passed the ball around until we became frustrated and came out of our normal defense. Once we started chasing them, they would attack the basket and beat us for easy layups. One of their guards, Doug Penno, was particularly damaging, scoring 9 points in the first half. That might not sound like much, but the score at halftime was 19-14, with Kettering leading.

That's right, our high-flying team, poised to win a national championship, had managed only 14 points in the first half.

Things weren't looking good. Going into the locker room, we were all thinking the same thing: *we cannot lose a championship game two years in a row.* That's exactly what you should *not* be thinking during halftime of a close game.

"Fellas," I said once we'd all gathered, "it's not about X's and O's right now. I want you to try and really grasp the opportunity that you have been given. Look around the room, guys. Some of you — Dru, LeBron, Sian, Romeo, Willie — will never play another game of basketball together again. Let's be real about this. To be where you guys are is a blessing that you will only understand later in life. This will probably be the last game where I coach some of you guys. We have experienced a lot of great times and tons of great memories. I'm going to cherish them. So let's do this. Let's end this thing the right way!"

I walked over to the board to review the strategy again. Something inside told me to stop. I turned. "Forget all this stuff. It's not about strategy right now — it's about what's inside here." With the palm of my hand, I patted my own chest.

As a team, we had to prove what was in our hearts. They

had just sixteen minutes to accomplish what they had dreamed about since fifth grade. This was their last chance to win a national championship. And they did ... together.

Our comeback started with a defensive switch. I put Dru on Penno, telling him to make defense his only priority in the second half.

"I don't care if you score another point," I said to my son. "Just shut him down."

The switch worked. With their top scorer neutralized, Kettering's offense began to lose its rhythm. As they lost their stride offensively, we began to find ours. With LeBron finding open teammates, we got back in the game and even opened up a 10-point lead. But championships are rarely blowouts, and this game proved no exception.

Kettering fought and clawed its way back into the game. In the waning seconds, the Knights even got off a three-pointer that would've tied it. They missed. We controlled the rebound. Moments later, we were champs.

The buzzer sounded. The scoreboard read: St. Vincent-St. Mary 40, Kettering 36.[*] Cheers erupted from all across the Value City Arena. The sound marked a monumental victory against a particularly tough opponent. But more important, our dream had at last come to fruition.

We all ran out onto that court in a huddle of celebratory relief. Our emotions ranged from euphoria to nostalgia. I wanted to say so many things, but I also wanted to etch into my mind this memory — to capture this moment forever. All we could do was laugh and cry. Holding one another, we threw our arms in the air and relished the moment.

---

[*] See Appendix A for box score.

When I hugged Dru, I held him close and whispered in his ear, "Don't ever give up on your dream. Just look at me."

My message was twofold:

1. I didn't want him to find himself in the middle of life wondering where he went wrong. I wanted my son, and all my kids, to learn from my experience and get it right from the start.
2. I wanted him to know dreams do come true. My childhood desire to become a coach happened. My son's dream to excel at basketball happened. We shared a dream. As hard as that was sometimes, the result was something beautiful.

After the game, the team came back home to a welcoming committee of massive crowds swarming the streets of Akron. We were greeted by camera crews and handmade signs singing our praises. People clapped, cheered, and recorded the historic event. Even the mayor came and spoke at the school.

In the high school corridors, everyone danced and celebrated and hugged one another. I had never witnessed this sense of euphoria before. Kids painted their faces and sprayed their hair green — all as a tribute to their beloved Fighting Irish. Yellow streamers hung from the ceiling of the school, like one giant party whose momentum seemed unstoppable.

And all of this because we dared to dream.

We had won the *USA Today* national championship. Soon after, *USA Today* would name me the coach of the year. Reading those headlines in the newspaper brought me a lot more satisfaction and joy than the ones I'd seen the previous year.

We had fought the good fight, finished the race, flipped our flop, and were alone on top.

Even though I am a man of serious faith, I have learned over the years that faith alone will only take you so far. As the Scripture puts it, "faith without works is dead."[39] While I had faith that I could thrive outside the comfortable confines of corporate America, I had to step out and work for it. My faith was only realized because I put tremendous effort into becoming a basketball coach, using my talents to build a business around the sport I had grown to love. In this way, I not only dared to dream, but I found a way to make my dream come true on terms that made sense to me and honored God.

Ultimately, no matter who you are, how old you are, what obstacle you have to overcome, where you live, or how hopeless you may feel — you can always take action.

This book isn't about basketball. I said it in the introduction, and I'm saying here at the end. But I'm leaving you with a final metaphor from the sport: think of each day of your life as the beginning of a game. You're standing at center court. The referee blows his whistle and throws the ball into the air. As you watch it rise to its apex, hold to the conviction that anything is possible. Anything.

BEYOND THE COURT

Question: What is your greatest dream in life? What obstacles stand in your way? What steps can you take in the next year to make it happen?

Question: What "coincidences" have come together in your life in a way you can't explain? Looking back, do you see God's guiding hand at work?

Question: Why does achieving a dream that you've had to work hard at feel better than something that's just handed to you? What does this teach you about life?

ACKNOWLEDGEMENTS

To Chris, thank you for believing in this project, at times more than I did. Your star is rising, and I'm grateful you have taken us along. To Monica, thank you for standing in the gap. Your work is much appreciated — more than words can say.

Special thanks to Kris Belman and Harvey Mason, two of the creative forces behind the acclaimed documentary *More Than a Game*. Without the documentary and the publicity tour, this book wouldn't have happened.

To Margaret and Erin at WME Entertainment, thank you for all your hard work in making my dream come true.

To John Sloan and the entire Zondervan team, thank you for believing I had something worth saying. I can't tell you how humbled I am that you would take a chance on a high school coach.

To my mother, father, and sister, JoAnne, who have all gone on to be with the Lord. Everything begins with you three in my life. I couldn't have asked for better parents or a more inspiring big sister. We miss you.

Special thanks to my daughters, Ursula and India. You shared me with so many people and never complained. But always remember — I coached you two first.

Special thanks to my sons, Dru III and Cameron, and to Bron, Sian, Willie, Romeo, and all my players, who are like sons to me. Space doesn't allow me to name all of you, but know that I've enjoyed the time we've spent together. It has been my honor to be involved in your lives. I continue to encourage all of you to never give up on your dreams. To the parents of my players, it has been a great ride. Sometimes the road has been bumpy, but you believed in me enough to let me be a part of your sons' lives, and for that I am eternally grateful.

To my father-in-law and mother-in-law, Reverend Cleo and Mildred Brooks, thank you for your daughter, my wife, Carolyn. She is everything you said she would be. Your prayers and help over the years mean more than you will ever know.

To my sons-in-law, David and Corey, and my daughters-in-law, Lanae and Devin, you are great additions to the family. Thank you for making my children complete and for your hard work in helping make our tournament business what it is today.

To my spiritual leaders — Bishop Joey Johnson, words can't say how much you've impacted my life; Pastor Richard Walker, my friend and discipler, miles and life have put distance between us, but my walk would not be the same without you. Robert "Mac" McFarland, my spiritual journey began with you. You are and have been a great friend. Chuck Swindoll, John Maxwell, Charles Stanley, your words have inspired me.

Special thanks to Kirk Linderman, Lee Cotton, James Tribble, Rick Bock, Percy Robinson, Brian Bachman, and the long list of travel team coaches. Your service to the kids touched by our program may go unnoticed by some, but your sacrifice will always be honored by me.

To Keith Dambrot and the STVM coaches I've had the privilege of sharing the sidelines with, thank you. We've done a great job building a dynasty that will not be forgotten. Brian

Knight and Dr. Mike Magoline, I've said many times that you guys, the STVM training staff, are the reason I stay. Thank you for your selfless service not only to my athletes but to all the athletes at STVM. Lee Wolf and Jim Sansonetti, you both have made my job easier. Thank you for all you do. Thanks to the Piglia family for your support.

Special thanks to Aaron Bachman, Kevin McIntyre, and Tina McIntyre. You make the King James tournaments successful. They wouldn't be what they are without you. You are always there for me, and I appreciate it.

To Mayor Don Plusquellic and the city of Akron's recreation department, thank you for your partnership and your help in making the King James Shooting Stars Classic the best travel team tournament in America.

To Patty Burdon and Ryan Thogmartin, your pictures capture the essence of STVM basketball. Thank you for your good work.

Last, but surely not least, thanks to the St. Vincent-St. Mary family for giving me a chance. I think we've done pretty good, I hope you do too.

STATE CHAMPIONSHIP BOX SCORES

Every year of the Fab Four's (then the Fab Five) high school basketball career, St. Vincent-St. Mary advanced to the state championship game. Here are the official box scores from each of those years.[40]

2000: BOYS DIVISION III STATE CHAMPIONSHIP

Game day: March 25
Game time: 5 p.m.
Venue: Value City Arena, Columbus, Ohio
Attendance: 13,061

Score by Quarter	1st	2nd	3rd	4th	Total
St. Vincent-St. Mary	17	13	25	18	73
Jamestown Greeneview	17	10	11	17	55

Visitors: Akron St. Vincent-St. Mary (27-0)

Name	Minutes	Points	Rebounds	Assists
Maverick Carter	25	6	3	2
Aly Samabaly	23	9	4	1
Chad Mraz	23	5	2	1
LeBron James	29	25	9	4
John Taylor	27	0	2	5
Dru Joyce III	10	21	0	1

Name	Minutes	Points	Rebounds	Assists
William McWain	1	0	0	0
Willie McGee	4	0	0	0
Lee Cotton	1	2	0	1
Jason Sherry	1	2	0	0
Jermeny Johnson	1	2	0	0
Sian Cotton	15	1	5	0

Home: Jamestown Greeneview (23-5)

Name	Minutes	Points	Rebounds	Assists
Berman Matthews	24	4	5	1
Josh Carter	24	12	5	0
Joe McClure	27	4	5	2
Gregg Haines	31	17	6	6
Trevor Thomas	30	9	5	0
Brent Gill	2	0	0	0
Marty Willis	1	2	0	0
Jeff Cardwell	1	0	0	0
Chris Bailey	3	0	0	0
Joe Pauley	16	5	1	0
Justin Earley	0+	0	0	0
Jeremy Crosswhite	1	2	0	0

2001: BOYS DIVISION III STATE CHAMPIONSHIP

Game day: March 24
Game time: 11 a.m.
Venue: Value City Arena, Columbus, Ohio
Attendance: 17,612

Score by Quarter	1st	2nd	3rd	4th	Total
St. Vincent-St. Mary	8	17	22	16	63
Casstown Miami East	17	9	12	15	53

Visitors: Akron St. Vincent-St. Mary (26-1)

Name	Minutes	Points	Rebounds	Assists
John Taylor	24	10	7	3
Sian Cotton	18	0	4	2
Aly Samabaly	28	12	8	1
Dru Joyce III	28	10	1	3
LeBron James	32	25	10	3
William McWain	3	0	0	0
Willie McGee	4	2	1	0
Jermeny Johnson	3	0	0	0
Jamie Cavileer	0+	0	0	0
Romeo Travis	19	4	3	0
Brandon Weems	1	0	0	0
Lee Cotton	0+	0	0	0
Josh Cavileer	0+	0	0	0

Home: Casstown Miami East (25-3)

Name	Minutes	Points	Rebounds	Assists
Travis Mumma	31	16	6	2
Zach Comer	23	4	5	1
Nathan Chivington	28	13	9	5
Paul Hershberger Jr.	31	4	1	3
Kenny Sandlin	29	13	3	0
Ryan Gray	0+	0	0	0
David Wagner	0+	0	0	0
Jason Sowry	4	0	0	0
John Young	0+	0	0	0
Dan Bentley	14	3	2	0
Andrew Armstrong	0+	0	0	0
Derek Mumma	0+	0	0	0

2002: BOYS DIVISION II STATE CHAMPIONSHIP

Game day: March 23

Game time: 11 a.m.

Venue: Value City Arena, Columbus, Ohio

Attendance: 18,375

Score by Quarter	1st	2nd	3rd	4th	Total
St. Vincent-St. Mary	17	13	16	17	63
St. Bernard Roger Bacon	15	16	20	20	71

Visitors: Akron St. Vincent-St. Mary (23-4)

Name	Minutes	Points	Rebounds	Assists
Sekou Lewis	25	2	1	1
Chad Mraz	32	4	3	1
Dru Joyce III	32	6	1	4
LeBron James	32	32	3	6
Romeo Travis	28	19	9	1
Corey Jones	4	0	0	0
Willie McGee	1	0	1	0
Sian Cotton	6	0	0	0

Home: St. Bernard Roger Bacon (25-3)

Name	Minutes	Points	Rebounds	Assists
Josh Hausfeld	32	23	7	6
David Johnson	32	3	1	3
Monty St. Clair	32	15	4	2
Beckham Wyrick	24	14	6	1
Frank Phillips	32	13	5	4
Leonard Bush	5	3	4	0
Jon Newton	3	0	1	0

2003: BOYS DIVISION II STATE CHAMPIONSHIP

Game day: March 22
Game time: 5 p.m.
Venue: Value City Arena, Columbus, Ohio
Attendance: 18,454

Score by Quarter	1st	2nd	3rd	4th	Total
Kettering Archbishop Alter	6	13	6	11	36
St. Vincent-St. Mary	8	6	13	13	40

Visitors: Kettering Archbishop Alter (18-9)

Name	Minutes	Points	Rebounds	Assists
Doug Penno	31	12	3	2
Andy Stichweh	31	4	5	1
Adam Gill	32	6	8	2
Jack Hilgeman	25	3	4	2
Eric Laumann	32	11	4	1
Bo Keyes	8	0	0	0
Zach Freshwater	1	0	0	0

Home: Akron St. Vincent-St. Mary (25-1)

Name	Minutes	Points	Rebounds	Assists
Romeo Travis	26	8	4	0
Sian Cotton	25	2	5	0
Corey Jones	25	5	1	0
Dru Joyce III	32	0	0	5
LeBron James	32	25	11	2
Brandon Weems	10	0	0	0
Willie McGee	8	0	1	0
Marcus Johnson	2	0	0	0

LEBRON JAMES' HIGH SCHOOL STATS

LeBron James proved early on that he was a once-in-a-generation talent. From the moment he stepped on the court as a freshman, he proved that he was destined for NBA greatness. Here are LeBron's season averages from each of his years at St. Vincent-St. Mary.[41]

FRESHMAN YEAR

Points per game:	18.0
Rebounds:	6.2
Assists:	3.6
Steals:	3.1
Blocks:	1.0
Turnovers:	2.1

Season Percentages

Field goal:	51.6 %
Three-point shooting:	31.6 %
Free throw:	79.7 %

SOPHOMORE YEAR

Points per game:	25.3
Rebounds:	7.4
Assists:	5.5
Steals:	3.7
Blocks:	1.6
Turnovers:	2.3

Season Percentages

Field goal:	58.4 %
Three-point shooting:	39.3 %
Free throw:	71.1 %

JUNIOR YEAR

Points per game: 28.0
Rebounds: 8.9
Assists: 6.0
Steals: 3.0
Blocks: 1.7
Turnovers: 3.3

Season Percentages
Field goal: 56.5 %
Three-point shooting: 34.0 %
Free throw: 59.3 %

SENIOR YEAR

Points per game: 30.4
Rebounds: 9.7
Assists: 4.9
Steals: 2.9
Blocks: 1.9
Turnovers: 2.8

Season Percentages
Field goal: 56.0 %
Three-point shooting: 38.2 %
Free throw: 67.8 %

HIGH SCHOOL CAREER TOTALS

Points: 2,657
Rebounds: 842
Assists: 523

NOTES

1. I owe a word of thanks to Pastor R.B. Thieme Jr., who used this phrase in a sermon I heard him preach on the biblical principle of sowing and reaping.

2. Riach, Steve, *True Heroes of Sports* (Nashville: Thomas Nelson, 2009), 124.

3. Roosevelt, Eleanor, *You Learn by Living: Eleven Keys for a More Fulfilling Life* (New York: HarperCollins, 1960, 2011), 130.

4. From sermon at The House of the Lord, Akron, Ohio.

5. Alina Tugend, "Praise Is Fleeting, But Brickbats We Recall," *The New York Times* (March 23, 2012): http://www.nytimes.com/2012/03/24/your-money/why-people-remember-negative-events-more-than-positive-ones.html?pagewanted=all&_r=0.

6. Letter from Isaac Newton to Robert Hooke, February 5, 1676.

7. Wooden, John with Jack Tobin, *They Call Me Coach,* (New York: The McGraw-Hill Companies, 2004), 95.

8. *They Call Me Coach,* 185.

9. Wooden, John and Steve Jamison, *The Wisdom of Wooden: My Century On and Off the Court* (New York: The McGraw-Hill Companies, 2010), 71.

10. Belman, Christopher, *More Than a Game* (Los Angeles: Lions Gate Entertainment, 2008).

11. Quote widely sourced to James Naismith, available in the article by Bill Self "Soul of Kansas: Naismith Provided Opportunity," *The Topeka Capital Journal* (October 22, 2011): http://cjonline.com/news/2011-10-22/soul-kansas-naismith-provided-opportunity.

12. *More Than a Game.*

13. Del Rey, Jason, "Maverick Carter, Founder of LRMR Innovative Marketing & Branding," *Inc.com* (July 19, 2010): http://www.inc.com/30under30/2010/profile-maverick-carter-lrmr-innovative-marketing-branding.html.

14. See Proverbs 27:6.

15. Cherner, Reid, "LeBron documentary: Q&A with coach Dru Joyce," *USA Today* (September 29, 2009): http://content.usatoday.com/communities/gameon/post/2009/09/68499943/1#.VApQU7-cDV0.

16. Stanley, Dr. Charles, "Discipline Determines Destiny," sermon outline, In Touch Ministries (2014): http://www.intouch.org/you/sermon-outlines/content?topic=discipline_determines_destiny_sermon_outline.

17. Arnovitz, Kevin, "The First Time LeBron Dunked a Basketball," *ESPN.com* (March 15, 2011): http://espn.go.com/blog/truehoop/miamiheat/post/_/id/5266/the-first-time-lebron-dunked-a-basketball.

18. MacMullan, Jackie, "Routine Excellence Is Allen's Secret," *The Boston Globe* (April 20, 2008): http://www.boston.com/sports/articles/2008/04/20/routine_excellence_is_allens_secret/?page=full.

19. "Routine Excellence Is Allen's Secret."

20. Wooden, John and Jay Carty, *John Wooden One-on-One* (Ventura, CA: Regal Books, 2003), 20.

21. Gladwell, Malcolm, *Outliers: The Story of Success* (New York: Little Brown and Company, 2008), 42.

22. *Outliers*, 150.

23. *More Than a Game.*

24. Dr. Martin Luther King, Jr., "Conquering Self-Centeredness," (August 11, 1957): http://mlk-kpp01.stanford.edu/primarydocuments/Vol4/11-Aug-1957_ConqueringSelf-Centeredness.pdf.

25. John Wooden popularized this phrase. He based it on one of his favorite maxims, "Much can be accomplished by teamwork when no one is concerned about who gets credit," from *Wooden: A Lifetime of Observations and Reflections on and off the Court,* 199.

26. Jordan, Michael. *I Can't Accept Not Trying* (San Francisco: HarperCollins, 1994).

27. James, LeBron and Buzz Bissinger, "LeBron's Band of Brothers," book excerpt, *Vanity Fair,* (September 2009): http://www.vanityfair.com/culture/features/2009/10/lebron-james200910#.

28. Withers, Tom, "Hummergate: LeBron Cleared," The Associated Press (January 28, 2003): http://www2.cincinnati.com/preps/2003/01/28/wwwprep2a28.html.

29. "Hummergate: LeBron Cleared."

30. *More Than a Game.*

31. Smith, Sam, "Making a Run From the Border," *Chicago Tribune* (February 17, 1998): http://articles.chicagotribune.com/1998-02-17/sports/9802170023_1_76ers-iverson-foreign-teams-nick-anderson.

32. Niebuhr, Reinhold, "Serenity Prayer," http://www.beliefnet.com/Prayers/Protestant/Addiction/Serenity-Prayer.aspx#.

33. Fox, Emily Jane, "Number of U.S. Millionaires Hits New High," *CNN Money* (March 14, 2014): http://money.cnn.com/2014/03/14/news/economy/us-millionaires-households.

34. See 2 Peter 1:5 – 7.

35. From sermon at The House of the Lord, Akron, Ohio.

36. Taylor, John, *The Rivalry: Bill Russell, Wilt Chamberlain, and the Golden Age of Basketball* (New York: Ballantine Books, 2006), 6.

37. Hughes, Langston, "Harlem," *Collected Poems* (the Estate of Langston Hughes, 1994): http://www.poetryfoundation.org/poem/175884.

38. Brennan, Eamonn, "ACC's Shot Clock Experiment: Why Not?" *ESPN.com* (May 15, 2014): http://espn.go.com/blog/collegebasketballnation/post/_/id/99012/accs-shot-clock-experiment-why-not.

39. Paraphrase of James 2:17 (NKJV).

40. Box scores from the Ohio High School Athletic Association: http://www.ohsaa.org/sports/bk/boys/pastresults.htm.

41. Burns, Ashley, "Check Out LeBron James' High School Stats," *Uproxx.com* (May 20, 2013): http://uproxx.com/sports/2013/05/check-out-lebron-james-high-school-stats.

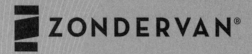

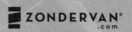